New Edition

Viewfinder

Topics

Resource Book

Gender Roles

by
Annegret Schrick

Langenscheidt

Berlin · München · Wien · Zürich · New York

Viewfinder

Topics

Resource Book

Gender Roles
Equal but Different?

Herausgeber:
Prof. em. Dr. Dr. h.c. mult. Peter Freese, Paderborn

Autorin:
StD Dr. Annegret Schrick, Gevelsberg

Projekt-Team:
Dr. Martin Arndt, Münster
David Beal, M. A., Bochum
Cornelia Becker, Bremen
Dr. Peter Dines, Cert. Ed., Ludwigsburg
Prof. i.R. Dr. Hanspeter Dörfel, Ludwigsburg
Prof. Dr. Sabine Doff, Frankfurt am Main
OStR Dieter Düwel, Castrop-Rauxel
Prof. em. Dr. Dr. h.c. mult. Peter Freese, Paderborn
Dr. Carin Freywald †
Jennifer von der Grün, B. A., Dortmund
OstR Ulrich Imig, Wildeshausen
OStR Reimer Jansen, Oyten-Sagehorn
Dr. Michael Mitchell, M. A., Reken und Warwick
Prof. Dr. Michael Porsche, Paderborn
StD i.E. Detlef Rediker, Lippstadt
StD Dr. Peter-J. Rekowski, Kirchhain
OStR i.K. Peter Ringeisen, M. A., Amberg
Karl Sassenberg, Münster
StD Henning Scholz †
StD Dr. Annegret Schrick, Gevelsberg
OStR Ekkehard Sprenger, Olympia, USA
OStD Dr. Dietrich Theißen †
Donald Turner, M. A. †
Prof. Dr. Laurenz Volkmann, Jena
Philip Wade, M. A., Cert. Ed., Amberg

Verlagsredaktion: Dr. Beatrix Finke

Layout und Produktion: kaltnermedia GmbH, Bobingen

Umwelthinweis: Gedruckt auf chlorfrei gebleichtem Papier.

1. Auflage 2007

© 2007 Langenscheidt ELT GmbH, München

Das Werk und seine Teile sind urheberrechtlich geschützt. Jede Verwertung in anderen als den gesetzlich zugelassenen Fällen bedarf deshalb der vorherigen schriftlichen Einwilligung des Verlages.

Printed in Germany

ISBN 978-3-526-50733-8

Contents

Course Manager .... p. 5
   The Theme .... p. 5
   The Students' Book .... p. 6
   Teaching Strategies .... p. 10
   Getting the Course Started .... p. 12
   Media .... p. 13

Teaching Resources .... p. 14

Gender Role Formation in Childhood and Adolescence .... p. 14

1 | Mark Twain: "Boy or Girl?"* .... p. 14
2 | Gender and the three R's: The development of literacy achievement by girls and boys* .... p. 16

Changing Roles of Women .... p. 20

3 | "The Seneca Falls Convention" .... p. 20
4 | William Congreve: "Battle of the Sexes"* .... p. 22
5 | "It is a truth universally acknowledged…": Jane Austen and the Marriage Market* .... p. 24
6 | Kate Chopin: "The Story of an Hour" .... p. 28

Changing Roles of Men .... p. 31

7 | William Brandon: "The Wild Freedom of the Mountain Men" ... p. 31
8 | Joolz: "Mammy's Boy" .... p. 33
9 | Peter Redgrove: "Early Morning Feed" .... p. 35
10 | "The myth of Super Dad" .... p. 36

Where Do We Go from Here? .... p. 39

11 | Fun Quiz: Are you hetero, metro or completely off the dial? ... p. 39
12 | "The new ladette or: Call my bluff?"* .... p. 42
13 | "A bad victory for women" .... p. 44
14 | Adriaane Pielou: "Prattle of the sexes" .... p. 46
15 | David Cohen: "A Gender for Change" .... p. 49

*Titles provided by the editor

Info Sheets

Info Sheet 1:	"Why She Became He"	p. 51
Info Sheet 2:	"What Little Girls Are Really Made of …"	p. 52
Info Sheet 3:	Role cards for role play on "Do we need girls' schools?"	p. 53
Info Sheet 4:	The Distillers, "Seneca Falls"	p. 54
Info Sheet 5:	Historical Development of the Women's Rights Movements in the U.S. and Britain	p. 55
Info Sheet 6:	Main Tendencies in the Women's Movement	p. 57
Info Sheet 7:	Suffragettes on Hunger Strike in Holloway	p. 58
Info Sheet 8:	The Diary of Samuel Pepys	p. 59
Info Sheet 9:	Role Cards	p. 60
Info Sheet 10:	Suggestions for the Restructuring of Work	p. 61
Info Sheet 11:	Glossary	p. 62
Info Sheet 12:	Nursery Rhymes	p. 64

Course Manager

The Theme

This *Viewfinder* volume, entitled "Gender Roles: Equal but Different?" is **not** (only) about women's rights; **not** (exclusively) about feminism; **not** (solely) about power struggle; it covers all of these aspects, plus many more, and tries to investigate into these sometimes delicate issues sensitively. After all, they concern all of us, personally. Everybody experiences gender roles and has to come to terms with the concomitant role expectations in some form or other. In this context people tend to think in binary oppositions: 'male' – 'female'; 'man' – 'woman'; 'boy' – 'girl' or 'identity' – 'otherness'. In the course of this investigation the aim is to find out when people first become conscious of these concepts, and who influences the ways they experience them; to try and allocate what proportion of our gender experience can be attributed to 'nature' and what to 'nurture'. "Gender Roles" does not only explore the role feminists[1] have played in this dichotomy, but also look at the male point of view in this highly controversial debate. In addition to that it draws attention to recent attitudinal, legal and linguistic changes and trends in social psychology. Speculation about the future development of gender roles is certainly a fascinating topic. Reading some of the more recent publications one must come to the conclusion that gender is a multi-faceted term the interpretation of which definitely depends on the ideology of the interpreter, but also on the social circumstances of a given historical context. In epistemological research it is now an acceptable theory to consider gender independent of sex.

"If gender is the cultural meanings the sexed body assumes, then a gender cannot be said to follow from a sex in any one way. Taken to its logical limit, the sex/gender distinction suggests a radical discontinuity between sexed bodies and culturally constructed genders. [...] When the constructed status of gender is theorized as radically independent of sex, gender itself becomes a free-floating artifice, with the consequence that *man* and *masculine* might just as easily signify a female body as a male one, and *woman* and *feminine* a male body as easily as a female one." [2]

If one looks ahead, it is only logical that one must also look back at how gender roles were defined in the past and how the incumbents of these roles felt about the role behaviour expected of them. The major changes in role behaviour for men and women must be stated as well as the preconditions on which those changes occurred.

This anthology contains four sections with a great variety of materials including expository and literary texts, which cover Britain and the U.S., as well as different historical periods so that the teacher can make optimum use of the opportunities offered by the curriculum.

The four sections are:
- **Gender role formation in childhood and adolescence:** On the basis of two texts and the anonymous nursery rhyme on p. 5 we look at what makes boys and girls 'tick' in childhood, what they play with and how they play, but also what possible encouragement is given to them by their parents and teachers.
- **Changing roles of women:** This section provides a lot of information about facts that many people either do not know or have not made clear to themselves, including the different legal treatment of men and women, and different business procedures (married women were not allowed to open bank accounts without consent).
- **Changing roles of men:** This section takes us from the myth of masculinity via the traditional role of the family man and protector to the concepts of men as sons and the heads of single-parent families.
- **Where do we go from here?** Despite a multitude of changes there are some areas which will not change: men and women experience their marriages differently; there will always be sexual harrassment; yet, in all those cases the crucial point is how men and women deal with those phenomena: as inducements for tolerance or strife. And in this context the last text must be seen as an attempt at bridging the gap between the sexes, as an 'agenda' for change.

---

[1] Betty Friedan, founder of the National Organization for Women (NOW) is quoted to have said, "Feminism is good for men." Possibly David Cohen, author of text 15, would agree with her.
[2] Judith Butler, *Gender Trouble. Feminism and the Subversion of Identity* (New York: Routledge, 1990), p. 6.

The Students' Book

The *Students' Book* consists of **15 texts**, representing the following text types: questionnaire, excerpt from a novel, short story, excerpt from a drama, pamphlet, song, poem, newspaper comment and newspaper report, scientific essay. There are also **50 thematically related illustrations**, ranging from photograph and poster to original drawing and cartoon.

The current *Richtlinien* demand that advanced EFL-courses pursue the aim of *Wissenschaftspropädeutik*, and contemporary EFL-methodology suggests that real life situations be brought into the classroom by means of 'authentic' texts. In compliance with these demands, the *Students' Book* presents each text in its original wording, marks omissions by [...] and titles provided by the editor with an *, and offers complete bibliographical data, which make it easy for the reader to check the contexts of the excerpts. Since an 'authentic' text is by definition one without annotations, each text is offered in an 'uncluttered' format, and the explanatory material is provided separately. The texts vary in difficulty from * (easily accessible) to *** (rather demanding) as defined by

- the number of unknown words,
- the syntactic complexity,
- the amount of background information required, and
- the intellectual level of the text.

The complete sequence progresses in a carefully structured way, but it is subdivided into four self-sufficient sub-sequences, each of which can be studied separately. This arrangement leaves it to the individual teacher to decide

- how many of these sub-sequences to deal with in a given course,
- in which order to introduce them, and
- whether to deal with them according to entirely different criteria.

  The *Students' Book* also offers
- 'vocabulary'– explanations of unknown words and phrases,
- 'explanations' – information about such 'culture-bound' ingredients as references to historical persons and events, place names, authors, titles, quotations, allusions, etc.,
- 'background information' on legal differences,
- 'extra information'– working definitions of such relevant concepts as 'Gender', 'Gender Socialization', 'Myth', etc.,
- biographical information about the authors,
- selected additional texts and illustrations, and
- carefully structured sets of questions and tasks.

These additional elements serve as both dictionary and encyclopaedia for the students and also provide elementary methodological guidelines for the teacher (see under "Teaching Strategies" for details).

The following synopsis provides an introductory survey of all texts and illustrations in the *Students' Book* with regard to their

- text type,
- length,
- degree of difficulty,
- theme, and
- teaching points.

Since this synopsis includes suggestions as to suitable teaching strategies and objectives for each sub-sequence, it enables the teacher to tailor the course to the needs of the students or learning-groups.

It should be stressed that individual teachers can, and should, begin the sequence with those texts which they feel will provide the best link to students' existing knowledge or previous work, or may be most appropriate in arousing their interest and enthusiasm. There are enough clear internal links within the sequence to construct logical progressions according to different criteria and resulting in a different order of texts from the one suggested here.

Sequence One: Gender Role Formation in Childhood and Adolescence

1 | Mark Twain "Boy or Girl?"*

text type: (extract from) novel
length: 821 words
degree of difficulty: **; 17 annotations, 2 explanations and 1 language note
theme: what makes the unpremeditated behaviour of girls different from that of boys? can this pattern be overcome consciously?
teaching points: narrative techniques

Huck and Jim on the Mississippi
photograph

2 | Gender and the three R's: The development of literacy achievement by girls and boys*

text type: expository text
length: 318 words
degree of difficulty: *; 7 annotations and 3 explanations
theme: standards of literacy among girls and boys
teaching points: sexual stereotypes

reading woman
photograph

The excerpt from *The Adventures of Huckleberry Finn* provides a suitable example of dealing with gender role formation in childhood and adolescence with the ironic twist that it does not only deal with the question "How do little girls/boys behave?", but with a boy imitating the behaviour of a girl. There is a Language note on p. 7 of the *Students' Book* to facilitate the reading of the excerpt.

The excerpt from the book *Language and Society* entitled "Gender and the three R's: The development of literary achievement by girls and boys"* introduces the reader into the vast field of 'literacy and gender' into which an enormous amount of research has recently been done. Differences in the reading and writing aptitude among boys and girls have been established and explained, even though a panacea has not been found yet.

The two texts which form the first mini-sequence alert the student to the concept of gender roles and to the interesting biographical period of adolescence. Background information on Gender socialization and Gender can be found on pp. 7 and 9 of the *Students' Book*.

Particular teaching points include techniques of narration, role behavior, aspects of the nature-nurture controversy, and sexual stereotypes.

In addition, the *Resource Book* contains optional Information Sheets:
Info Sheet 1:   "Why She became He"
Info Sheet 2:   "What Little Girls Are Really Made Of"
Info Sheet 3:   Role Cards for Role Play on: "Do We Need Girls' Schools?"
Info Sheet 12:   Nursery Rhymes

Sequence Two: Changing Roles of Women

3 | "The Seneca Falls Convention"

text type: historical pamphlet
length: 915 words
degree of difficulty: ***; 45 annotations and 1 explanation
theme: the first equal rights convention ever and the beginning of the woman's rights movement in the U.S.
teaching points: political register; important documents of U.S. history; discrimination against women in U.S. history

The second class status of women (U.S.)
historical poster

What a woman may be ... (GB)
historical poster

Did You Know (Noteworthy Dates)
collage

4 | William Congreve "Battle of the Sexes"*

text type: (extract from) drama
length: 1140 words
degree of difficulty: ***; 116 annotations and 5 explanations
theme: the stipulations of a marriage contract in the 17th century
teaching points: drama; legal aspects of marriage; rhetoric

drawing of a scene from a contemporary play

5 | "It is a truth universally acknowledged ...": Jane Austen and the Marriage Market

text type: (extract from) novel
length: 594 words
degree of difficulty: **; 25 annotations
theme: a rejected proposal
teaching points: analysis of novel; verbal and non-verbal behaviour; the marriage market as an apt metaphor of gender role difficulties; the landed gentry in 18th century in England

2 stills from 2005 film version
photos

Basildon Park (film location)
photo

6 | Kate Chopin "The Story of an Hour"

text type: short story (complete)
length: 981 words
degree of difficulty: **; 27 annotations and 1 explanation
theme: a Victorian marital relationship
teaching points: analysis of short story; the concept of the objective correlative; creation of suspense

woman in an armchair
watercolor

The second sequence covers a period of the past in which the changing roles of women became clearly noticeable. It begins with a historical document on the "Seneca Falls Convention" to draw attention to its importance as a historical landmark in women's fights for equal rights and opportunities. It is supplemented by background information on the early **American Women's Rights Movement** on p.15 and the anonymously issued **Invitation to the Convention** on p. 11 of the *Students' Book*.

This is juxtaposed by a scene from the Restoration drama "The Way of the World", in which a strong, independent woman lays down conditions for a marriage contract, before she even considers getting married. Needless to say, she is a woman of means. The excerpt is supplemented by background information on the **Restoration** (the period in which the drama is set) on p. 18 and how the topic of **Marriage** is generally treated by Restoration dramatists on p. 19 of the *Students' Book*.

In the excerpt from *Pride and Prejudice* the reader meets an equally strong woman in Elizabeth Bennet, but without the financial means. That is the reason why she puts herself at great risk, when she turns down Mr Darcy's first offer of marriage.

The materialization of gender roles in marital relationships is exemplified in "The Story of an Hour" which deals with the unexpected reactions of a wife to the news of her husband's death. Historically, it casts some light on the role of a wife in Victorian times in the U.S. It should also be seen in conjunction with the excerpt from "The Seneca Falls Convention" (text 3), since both texts were published roughly in the same period and could be seen as reflecting a similar problem on the basis of different text types: one as a fictional representation and the other as a historical document.

Particular teaching points include the vocabulary of sociology and the law, elements of drama and novel and rhetorical devices.

Relevant Information Sheets are provided in the *Resource Book*:

Info Sheet 4: "Seneca Falls" (Song by the Australian punk band 'The Distillers')
Info Sheet 5: Historical Development of the Women's Rights Movements in the U.S. and Britain
Info Sheet 6: Main Tendencies in the Women's Movement
Info Sheet 7: Suffragettes on Hunger Strike in Holloway
Info Sheet 8: The Diary of Samuel Pepys

Sequence Three: Changing Roles of Men

7 | William Brandon "The Wild Freedom of the Mountain Men"

text type: expository text (extract from travel writing)
length: 757 words
degree of difficulty: **; 47 annotations and 7 explanations
theme: the 'lone wolf' travelling alone and coping with danger
teaching points: the myth of masculinity; concepts of freedom

lone cowboy on a horse
inlay, photo

mountain man with his dog
photo

8 | Joolz "Mammy's Boy"

text type: song
length: 276 words
degree of difficulty: *; 11 annotations
theme: mother-son relationship
teaching points: structure of a song; tone in which it is presented; men as sons

Mother's Eternal Presence
cartoon

9 | Peter Redgrove "Early Morning Feed"

text type: poem
length: 186 words
degree of difficulty: *; 21 annotations
theme: father-son relationship
teaching points: aspects of poetry, imagery; evocation of feelings

baby in a cot
photo

10 | "The myth of Super Dad"

text type: newspaper article (feature story)
length: 1041 words
degree of difficulty: **; 36 annotations, 11 explanations
theme: a tongue-in-cheek account of New Labour's attempt at promoting new fatherhood; different types of male gender roles

Tony Blair with his baby
photo

"Paternity Leave"
cartoon

In his travelogue *The Men and the Mountain*, William Brandon presents the conventional image of the hero in the wilderness, fighting against the forces of nature. In this text the myth of masculinity is exemplified by the mountain man and his peers. The question of his socialization must be raised: how would a man like him cope in society?

Joolz' song presents man in the role of a son, dominated by his possessive mother. The song and the poem "Early Morning Feed" should be seen in conjunction with each other, not only for structural reasons. Both texts deal with

Gender Roles – Resource Book

very similar relationships: mother-son and father-son, but from radically different points of view.

In the excerpt from the newspaper article "The myth of Super Dad" the reader is given an overview from the New Man of the 1980s to the Super Dad of the new millennium. The policies of new fatherhood promoted by Tony Blair's Labour government form a political background foil.

Particular teaching points include the creation of myths in past and present everyday attitudes, aspects of semiotics, traits of domination, subordination and compromise in gender relationships, aspects of poetry (and songs), in particular the function of imagery. Background information on the role the **Mountain Men** played in history and on **Myth** is given in the *Students' Book* on pp. 31f., and on **Bonding** and **Momism** on pp. 34f.

Sequence Four: Where Do We Go from Here?

11 | Fun Quiz: Are you hetero, metro or completely off the dial?

text type: (newspaper) quiz/questionnaire
length: 1024 words
degree of difficulty: ***; 20 annotations; 28 explanations
theme: recent trends in male gender roles
teaching points: (gender) patterns in questionnaires; role expectations; British popular culture

- well-groomed man
  photo

- surfer
  photo

- recent trends in gender roles
  2 cartoons

12 | "The new ladette or: Call my bluff?"

text type: newspaper article (interpretive news story)
length: 1036 words
degree of difficulty: **, 36 annotations; 11 explanations;
theme: a personally teinted description of changed behavioral patterns among contemporary British young women
teaching points: reasons for and causes of behavioral patterns; role expectations; pc English; irony; style in newspaper articles

- Hen behaving badly
  cartoon

13 | "A bad victory for women"

text type: newspaper article (feature story)
length: 1114 words
degree of difficulty: **; 32 annotations and 5 explanations
theme: sexual harassment
teaching points: work ethics; irony; elements of subjective argumentation; reactions to (sexual) harassment

- equal payment
  2 cartoons

- car advertisement with graffiti
  poster

- board meeting
  cartoon

14 | Adriaane Pielou "Prattle of the sexes"

text type: newspaper article (feature)
length: 870 words
degree of difficulty: *; 32 annotations and 1 explanation
theme: gender-based language difference
teaching points: socio-linguistic aspects in the gender discussion; psychology of men and women

- Book cover: *You Just Don't Understand*

15 | David Cohen "A Gender for Change"

text type: expository text
length: 784 words
degree of difficulty: **; 34 annotations and 2 explanations
theme: male responses to recent feminist challenges
teaching points: losses and gains for men and women in their working and private lives; principles of job sharing; agenda for change

- happy couple
  photo

- car advertisement with graffiti
  poster

In the Fun Quiz: Are you hetero, metro or completely off the dial?, four types of modern men are introduced. It gives an entertaining touch to recent trends and takes the reader away from the dichotomy of 'male' vs. 'female' by offering different choices.

The excerpt from the interpretive news story "The new ladette or: Call my bluff?"* deals with the recent trend among British women to reveal blokish behaviour and also the peer pressure exerted on them. Texts 11 and 12 complement each other very well, as they draw attention to trends among men and among women. They are both accompanied by three cartoons on pp. 45, 46 and 48 in which the new role behaviour is presented in a satirical way. Background information on **Lad culture and ladette culture – British boys and girls gone wild** is given on p. 49.

The feature story "A bad victory for women" deals with a Wall Street banker who sued her employers for sexual harassment and won a massive compensation. The author claims, however, that the banker's behavior has been detrimental to sisterhood. Background Reading 1 on pp. 53f. gives information about **Sexual harassment** and Background Reading 2 on pp. 54f. deals with **Equality at work**. The Info box on p. 55 provides information about **Sexism**.

"Prattle of the sexes" – the title of text 14 – is almost self-explanatory, if one reads the text as a continuation of text 4. It deals with some psychological foundations of gender-specific linguistic behaviour. Linguistic differences based on gender have been covered extensively in research in recent years.

David Cohen strikes a conciliatory note when he makes up a losses and gains list for both genders. He admits that men have gained a lot from the changes feminists have succeeded in bringing about.

Particular teaching points include aspects of the analysis of newspaper articles and other non-literary texts, aspects of psycho- and sociolinguistics, and textual irony.

The *Resource Book* offers thematically relevant Information Sheets:
Info Sheet 10: Suggestions for the Restructuring of Work
Info Sheet 11: Glossary

To sum up: The first sequence is not only the shortest, but also the easiest, linguistically as well as conceptually. At the same time it is closest to the students' personal range of experience. For all these reasons it ideally serves the purpose of an introduction. The following three sequences are longer, and linguistically more demanding; they continue the discussion on a higher level of abstraction. Some knowledge of the registers of sociology and psychology is necessary and access to them has been provided.

It should be stressed again at this point that although there is a logical progression in the order of the texts as they stand, each sequence can successfully be dealt with as a self-contained unit and the order of the sequences is a matter for the individual teacher to decide. Nor is it essential to deal with every text within a sequence. In accordance with differing interests, different strands might be pursued.

In other words, the *Students' Book* and the *Resource Book* provide a wide range of carefully related building blocks which can be combined in numerous ways to suit the specific needs of any given course. The texts and illustrations are complemented by carefully chosen tasks and additional material. The further reading suggestions are not to be understood as a bibliography but as a selection of longer texts which offer special insights, are accessible to ordinary readers, and are central to the issues presented in this volume.

The Info Sheets in the *Resource Book* can either be used by the teacher to help in lesson preparation or can be photocopied and handed out to the students for individual presentations, group work or general information.

Particular teaching points include aspects of short story analysis, the creation of atmosphere, the concept of the objective correlative, aspects of psycho- and socio-linguistics, and textual irony.

Teaching Strategies

One of the main objectives is, obviously, to create awareness of and arouse curiosity for gender-specific issues. In this context it may be a great help that the issues can be or have been experienced by students in their immediate environment. If students are to report on and discuss their own experiences, a lot of tact is required, but in an anxiety-free atmosphere this should not be a problem.

- Students are to be made aware that they live in a gender-orientated environment, the – frequently unreflected – behavioral patterns of which go back into childhood.
- Given an acuter degree of awareness, students might reflect on their own behaviour and that of others on a higher level of abstraction.
- Students are to realize that the discussion of gender-specific topics is frequently charged with emotion and based on prejudice. – Students are to be familiarized with the necessary registers to discuss gender-specific issues.
- Students are to recognize that the concepts are not new, but go back to the roots of humanity.
- Students are to be alerted to the cultural, social and historical implications of gender-specific issues.

The successful exploration of the interplay between the foreign-language text and its cultural and historical context presupposes considerable knowledge, and that is why the *Resource Book* stresses the 'what' rather than the 'how' of teaching these materials, providing short but detailed commentaries on each text in essay form and confining itself to a few suggestions on particular teaching strategies.

Every practising teacher knows, better than educational theorists, that any theoretical scheme, however valuable, must be modified to suit the needs of individual learners and learning-groups (and the personality of the teacher). It is part of a teacher's training to recognize and evaluate the factors which need to be taken into account. Thus traditional teachers' books which progress from theoretical considerations, however well-founded, to assumptions about what takes place in class will inevitably restrict the parameters of interaction between the teacher and learner and rob the relationship of its necessary flexibility. The result may well be a boring lesson.

It can be assumed that practising EFL-teachers will be aware of the range of approaches and techniques designed to allow reflection, provoke discussion and promote understanding. Regular reappraisals of the most effective and appropriate methods of achieving these aims are a feature of educational publications. It would be a mistake to bind the presentation of the material given here to any one technique to the exclusion of others which might come to be recognized in the future.

Among commonly used approaches to texts it might be worth mentioning the following:
- 'reflective' individual reading involving deduction of meaning from contexts,
- general 'brainstorming' sessions,
- pair or group work involving interaction or 'sparking' of ideas,
- role-play,
- mind-mapping in branching diagrams,
- multi-media presentation,
- use of acting, mime, music, dance, etc.,
- distribution of individual lines of poems for 'free association',
- reassembling texts from fragments.

In the process of analysis, besides techniques involving division and connection, active strategies of parallel production (in the form of creative writing) may prove highly effective.

In any event, the *Viewfinder* concept sets out a basic scheme to make course work easier for students and teachers alike and provide a kind of base guideline for classroom activities and suitable homework. Thus the study aids contain questions and tasks for each text, which are, of course, offered with the tacit understanding that it is not necessary to deal with all of them, but that it is for the teacher and students to decide which ones they want to work on and how to go about it. Each set of tasks is structured in five or six phases, guiding students from an opening phase meant to create an initial awareness of the text via comprehension and analysis to a formulation of personal opinions and, in most cases, additional projects and suggestions for further reading to encourage independent activity.

Awareness

Awareness tasks are pre-reading tasks, which in a more student-centred approach to teaching in the EFL-classroom are of crucial importance, since they have the function of preparing the student for the reading process plus all other stages of involvement required in the different sets of tasks. They may help students to overcome the linguistic, cultural, historical and gender distances that a text involves.

Pre-reading tasks "are not designed to be self-contained. Their purpose is to direct attention to a text [...] in order to sensitise students to ideas and themes [...] and to encourage students to relate them to their own experience."[3]

Pre-reading tasks can also make students aware of their previous knowledge (or lack of it), recognize their expectations and prejudices, and increase the scope of their imagination as they approach a new text. In fact, they are designed to make reading – in the widest sense of the word – *pleasurable* for students.

The teacher will be able to gauge which, if any, pre-reading tasks are most appropriate for a particular group or individual, but separate sections with suggestions have been included in the detailed Teaching Resources section.

Comprehension

It is naturally essential to understand the linguistic and cultural elements in a text before forming any judgements about it. For this purpose 'vocabulary' and cultural or historical 'explanations' have been given. They are, however, separated from the text so that it is possible to train students in the use of appropriate single-language dictionaries or in the deduction of meanings from the context. As 'comprehension' in this limited sense is a precondition of textual analysis it does not receive attention in the *Resource Book*. The questions can be used to help students organise their ideas and allow the teacher to check wether the students have 'understood' the text and thereby achieve what German EFL-methodology calls *Sicherung des Textverständnisses*.

Analysis

The ability to analyse a text plays a central role in the requirements of the *Abitur*. A text cannot be fully understood at a cursory reading, which is why the analysis

---

[3] Ronald Carter and Michael N. Long, *Teaching Literature* (London: Longman, 1991), p. 22.

of what it says and how it does so extends understanding and is the basis the student's interaction with the text. Both the *Textaufgabe* and the *Themaaufgabe* as defined in the *Einheitliche Prüfungsanforderungen in der Abiturprüfung (EPA)* require the students to demonstrate their ability not only to comprehend but also to analyse the text. In keeping with the *Viewfinder* approach this is not limited to intrinsic aspects of the text, but involves its social and cultural context. For this phase, too, 'analysis' questions and tasks are provided.

Opinion

The object of this phase is for students to be able to form a considered opinion, rather than voicing an unconsidered reaction or prejudice. Students will take account of the new facts with which they have been confronted and express their view in appropriate language, individually or through negotiation or discussion. The 'opinion' questions are designed to guide students towards this ability.

Projects

It is often desirable to go beyond the analysis of a text and the formulation of a view to explore related fields, carry out research or initiate an activity in the form of a project. This can involve further individual work or group activity for which the individuals or groups take further responsibility. It is a type of work offering scope for variety, flexibility, and individual initiative and deepens the sense of involvement with the material. It also lends itself naturally to communicative activities like role-play, etc.. Suggestions for 'projects' are given in the *Students' Book* (although these, of course, are not exhaustive) and the *Resource Book* provides further material to help in carrying them out.

Suggested Further Reading

For students who are motivated to extend their reading horizons some suggestions have been included as encouragement. The suggestions can also be used for written or oral book reports, and to carry out further research into the vast field of gender studies. In addition, teachers might need suitable material for *Klausuren* which could be found in the works suggested.

To sum up, the questions and tasks for each text can be regarded as an elementary guideline, which can be varied and combined with other materials in the *Students' Book* and optional Information Sheets from the *Resource Book*. It constitutes a self-contained and complete introduction to the topic which can be taught without additional research or materials.

Getting the Course Started

There are as many different ways to get the course started as there are teachers to teach it:

Issues in the news might provide a good starting-point: when the media drew attention to the fact that members of the Anglican Church are now officially allowed to imagine God as a woman, this would have made a wonderfully controversial starting-point. From there an easy line could be drawn to the motivating simulated "Child's Letter to God" on p. 5, which, incidentally, ties up with the ideas of the Anglican Church.

Alternatively, one could envisage various forms of brainstorming sessions: from the very open form of "What characteristics do you associate with boys/girls, men/women?" to a more channelled version "A day in the life of ...", which could be completed by "A day in the life of a woman/man in the 19th century;" "A day in the life of a boy/girl in 2007."

Another speculation task would be to ask male students to slip into the role and clothes of a woman, and female students to slip into the role and clothes of a man for one day and to imagine what it would be like, and where they would foresee difficulties in their role behaviour.

Other teachers might prefer to start with an experiment. They could ask their female (male) students to write a story for a male (female) student.[4] A discussion of the stories and of the question whether students would find it easier to write for someone of the same sex could provide a fruitful introduction into the topics of sequence 1.

Another alternative could simply be to start with the fun quiz: "Are you hetero, metro or completely off the dial?" (text 11)

Others might want to start with a linguistic approach: students could compile a list of words that reveal the gender bias of the English language (man-made; overmanning; manslaughter; odd-man-out; the man in the street; chairman; manhandle; etc.). The following example is (not only) linguistically revealing, too. A male painter is quoted to have said about a female colleague: "When she's good, we call her a painter; when she's bad, we call her a lady painter." It is a truism that when contrasted semantically to the male form, the female term will also attract negative or unflattering associations.[5]

---

[4] See Janet White, "On Literacy and Gender", in: *Knowledge about language and the curriculum*, ed. by Ronald Carter (London: Hodder & Stoughton, 1990), p. 194.

[5] Margaret Atwood, "Paradoxes and Dilemma, the Woman as Writer," *Feminist Literary Theory*, ed. by Mary Eagleton (Oxford: Blackwell, 1986), p. 76, calls this phenomenon: the lady painter syndrome.

Media

The books mentioned in the introductions and biographical data or in the 'Suggested further reading' sections of the *Students' Book* or on the Information Sheets of the *Resource Book* are usually available in paperback and can be obtained from booksellers and mail-order firms.

The topic also lends itself to experiences of role expectations and behaviour in other media. Both the *Amerika-Haus* and the *British Council* offer a wide selection of well-known films on video, which can be used as introductions or illustrations for the topics. This selection includes a number of non-fictional videos under the heading of 'Feminism'.

The *British Council* also has a *Current Awareness File* entitled *Women* with newspaper clippings from the leading British national newspapers on offer.

According to the interests and knowledge of the teacher and/or group, or contacts made with people from a gender-relevant background, th following areas might be considered:
- CDs with interviews and lectures,
- CDs with poetry-reading and music
- slides and pictures of gender role behaviour 'in action'.

Teaching Resources

Gender Role Formation in Childhood and Adolescence

1 | Mark Twain "Boy or Girl?"*

text type: (extract from) novel
length: 821 words
degree of difficulty: **; 17 annotations and 2 explanations; language note
theme: what makes the unpremeditated behavior of girls different from that of boys? can this be overcome consciously?
teaching points: narrative techniques

related visual material: photograph of Huck and Jim on the Mississippi

for extra information on the language see *Students' Book*, p. 7;

The extract from *The Adventures of Huckleberry Finn* provides an apt and amusing episode in which a boy poses as a girl by wearing girls' clothing.

Background

Having gone through the preceding stage, students will presumably be aware of what to look for in the excerpt. Perhaps they are familiar with the novel, and if they are, they will probably have read it from a completely different point of view, possibly as a piece of adolescent literature, or a story of initiation. Literary criticism has, as is to be expected, voiced different opinions about the characters in the book, one of which is that "[they] are (in Whitman's words) 'refreshing, wicked, real'. Some of them, it is true, are caught in apathetic squalor, in small-town brutality, in meaningless blood-feuds, or (like Jim) in Negro slavery. But Huck himself is still free, the natural being not yet moulded and ruined by an environment that seeks to civilize him. He is able to free Jim from the immediate evil of slavery, though not from the disability of being black. But at the end Huck [...] must get away from civilization if he is to save himself."[6] Later, however, it becomes dramatically obvious that Huck is not as free as he believes himself to be, but conditioned by a slave-owner society. This leads to Huck's moral conflict of loyalties.

---

[6] Marcus Cunliffe, *The Literature of the United States* (Harmondsworth: Penguin, 1954), p. 176.

Awareness

In the context of this anthology, however, the discussion of this excerpt will focus on gender-specific behavior. The experiment with throwing a tennis ball into a boy's and a girl's lap may turn into an interesting revelation about different forms of gender-specific behavior, which might catch students unawares. Should you find out that students behave differently from the spontaneous behavior described in the episode from *The Adventures of Huckleberry Finn* it will offer a wonderful opportunity to discuss the differences and speculate on the reasons for them. Is it because young people these days dress differently, or is it because they have not been brainwashed into gender-specific physical behavior?

If students have a brainstorming session about different toys and later compare their results in class this will serve more than one purpose: students ought to become aware that children play with different toys at a fairly 'innocent' age. There can only be two explanations for this phenomenon: either boys and girls have genetically different codes which make them behave in an unpremeditated way or they have role models to emulate. In the latter case, social factors predominantly influence the child's behavior. This is, no doubt, a first introduction to the nature-nurture controversy, which in developmental psychology deals with the problem of ascribing due weight to genetic facts on the one hand and environmental ones on the other as factors responsible for the characteristics of an organism. The conflict roots in the nativist theory that perceptual or other faculties are innate and not dependent on experiential stimuli or reinforcement for their development. The additional material on p. 9 of the *Students' Book* provides more information on 'nature v. nurture.'

The Text

The excerpt from the novel presents an episode in which the orphaned Huck, dressed in girls' clothes, pretends to be a girl because as a runaway apprentice he is afraid that he will be returned to the authorities, if he is caught. He would then be sent back to his cruel master. Unfortunately, and naively, Huck has only thought about disguising himself, but not about the appropriate behavior that is part of being a girl.

The old lady, however, is instinctively suspicious, a feeling which is enhanced when the 'girl' does not remember her name correctly. When she throws a lump of lead into the 'girl's' lap and the 'girl' claps her knees together, the old lady's suspicion is confirmed: girls do not clap their knees together, but throw them apart, if they want to catch something in their lap. This experiment is prepared for by the incident in which they aim at some rats: girls tend to raise themselves on tiptoe, throw with a stiff arm from the shoulder and – this is the ultimate proof – miss the target (which is exactly what the old lady does herself).

One important aspect of the relationship between Huck and the old woman is the age difference between the two interlocutors: Huck's respect for the older person becomes quite obvious from his polite choice of words (e.g. "yes'm," l. 12), whereas the old lady's liking of the younger person is revealed in terms of endearment (e.g. "honey," l. 3). The old lady is much more experienced in life: she senses that Huck is there under false pretences. So she plays his game for a little while to make him feel at ease, but then she wants him to let his defenses down ("Come now – What's your real name?", l. 48). In general, however, the relationship between Huck and the old lady is rather strained, on the one hand because Huck is terrified of recognition and on the other hand because the old lady is suspicious of her visitor and feels cheated by 'her'. But after her suspicion has been confirmed, and Huck has no option but to reveal himself to her, she becomes quite friendly and sympathetic. She even offers him her help.

In this contest between trust and distrust the paralinguistic behavior of Huck and the old lady is just as important as what they say. Huck's avoidance of his interlocutor's eyes (ll. 6, 17) indicates that he feels ill at ease, even cornered (l. 7). Suspicious looks are cast to check out the interlocutor (l. 1). There is a contrast between the old lady's calmness and Huck's fidgeting anxiety ("the longer she set still, the uneasier I was," ll. 9f.). The showdown occurs when the lady looks him straight in the eye and asks a very direct embarrassing question, which makes him shake like a leaf (l. 52).

This paralinguistic behavior is paralleled by alternating reactions of talk and silence. Some silences are too long and almost unbearable for Huck (ll. 8f.), who is extremely anxious when she says very little, and feels completely reassured when her talk flows freely and naturally. He does not seem to realize that this is one of her devices to fool him into believing that she 'is buying' his story. Huck, on the other hand, does not say very much, his answers are curt and evasive in order not to give his game away. He stammers several times. In the end, to "make a clean breast" he confesses his entire story, when he sees that there is no other way out.

The first-person singular point of view is an ideal means of presenting Huck's emotional situation and the changing flow of his feelings. He minutely reports on his emotions, e.g. "I was feeling better then" (l. 16) or "I got easy again" (l. 21), but also seems to be conscious of what effect his reactions have on the old lady ["... so I felt sort of cornered, and was afeared maybe I was looking it, too" (ll. 7f.)]. Huck's behavior is typical of many people who try to dissimulate. There is often a mismatch between their intended pretence and the effect they have on the observer.

The first-person singular point of view, at the same time, prevents the reader from looking into the old lady's psyche, of course. This narrative technique is designed to maintain the level of suspense by presenting the narrative through Huck's eyes. Together with the protagonist, the reader tries to gauge the old lady's reactions. Even though the episode is rather short, the relative psychological experience of time differs according to Huck's emotions: when he is anxious, time does not seem to pass at all (which can be seen from the observations that go through his mind), but when he is lulled into feeling at ease, time seems to run at its normal speed. For all these reasons the reader can empathize much better with Huck and feel his varying degrees of panic and, finally, relief.

One can easily imagine that the old lady will appeal to her husband to help Huck, because in the contest of trust and distrust it becomes quite obvious that she basically likes Huck, which is stated quite openly later (ll. 58f.).

If one were to apply the information from the additional material, one could say that this episode shows a victory of nature over nurture. Huck behaves in accordance with his real identity. He has been naive enough to think that he can fool people by just wearing girls' clothing, and has not considered different forms of gender-specific behavior. Only conscious simulation could have overcome those gender barriers to a certain degree.

Students giving a written evaluation of the nature-nurture controversy could argue dialectically: one school of thought has it that the genetic make-up of a person is fixed and irreversible. It determines people's behavior and skills without any freedom of choice. Children who are mentally handicapped are genetically deficient. On the other hand, it has been revealed that the environment and social conditioning are of the utmost importance. That is why, e.g., feral children who grow up without any nurture are not to develop their genetically inherited capacities. It is also a fallacy to believe that genetically inherited traits are by definition unmodifiable. Human beings are not compelled to obey their genes all their lives, especially not those which exert a negative or harmful influence. Culture and influences which are learned or handed down offer a choice.

From the beginning of this century, the nature-nurture debate has also left its mark on empirical gender studies. "Does biology determine destiny and are men and women so very different in every respect: intellectually, emotionally and in terms of their social relationships and careers? Alternatively, are they similar creatures falsely presumed to be ideally biologically equipped for a variety of non-interchangeable sex-linked roles?"[7] Given these theoretical choices, differences in behavior between men and women were usually attributed to nature or biology. Women's superiority in verbal skills and men's in spatial skills and abstract reasoning as well as aggressiveness were most frequently emphasized. Feminist thinking from the late 60s has stressed, with equal conviction, the social context and the conditioning of sex-role behavior to explain observed differences between men and women.

A cautious consensus in the nature-nurture debate was arrived at in the mid-70s. On the basis of empirical research it was revealed that sex differences in behavior had been systematically exaggerated, and similarities minimized. There were no consistent sex differences in traits like achievement motivation, sociability, suggestibility, self-esteem and cognitive styles. Researchers did, however, privilege biological explanation over cultural explanation when it came to explaining differences in verbal and spatial ability, mathematical reasoning and aggressiveness. The psychological search for innate differences between the sexes has continued. One new area of research has been work on the asymmetry between the hemispheres of the brain. Yet, results have not been entirely convincing. The only consistent picture obtained from psychological sex-difference research is that sex-differences are small, their origins unclear, and the variation within each sex far outweighs differences between the sexes. Possibly, the nature-nurture concept is inadequate and theoretically simplistic.[8]

2 | Gender and the three R's: The development of literacy achievement by girls and boys*

text type: expository text
length: 318 words
degree of difficulty: *; 7 annotations and 3 explanations
theme: standards of literacy among girls and boys
teaching points: sexual stereotypes

related visual material: photograph of a reading woman

The Context

In the period of adolescence the young person leaves behind the phase of protective childhood and at the same time finds an identity in the realm of gender. This process seems to have become more difficult in an increasingly complex world, and may even lead to neurotic difficulties of adjustment. Even though socialisation (the process whereby the biological being is transformed into a specific cultural being) is intended to make human beings safe, adolescents tend to be insecure, "never quite certain whether they will be admitted to the world of the dominant adults. [...] To make a mature adjustment one has to belong to a *definite* world."[9] Adolescents, however, frequently feel as if they were marginal beings.

In this period of life, role models are even more important than at any other time of a person's psychological and social development. Adolescents are frequently confronted with their role models in the literature they read at school or at home. That is why another facet of the nature-nurture controversy is that of literacy and gender. "Boys are more to do with practical work and experiments and girls are more to learn and listen and enjoy writing." This comment made by a 15-year-old boy[10] could be seen as a truism not only for British and American schools. In the 80s an enormous amount of research was carried out into gender differences in literacy. One of the more surprising results was that not only are boys less proficient concerning their degree of literacy, but they make up for it by their sheer volume of talk. "One of the abiding ironies in the present schooling ethos is that for all the public and professional promotion of 'literacy' as the touchstone of educational success, in the day-to-day encounters of the classroom it is the quiet girl reading and writing with untroubled competence who is thought to be merely passive and probably dull, while

---

[7] Yvette Walczak, *He and She: Men in the Eighties* (London: Routledge, 1988), quoted in Lynne Segal, *Slow Motion: Changing Masculinities. Changing Men* (London: Virago, 1990), p. 61.

[8] Some texts discussing the nature-nurture controversy in the realm of gender studies: Ruth Bleier, *Science and Gender: A Critique of Biology and Its Theories on Women* (London: Pergamon Press, 1984); B. Lloyd/J. Archer (eds.), *Exploring Sex Differences* (London: Academic Press, 1976); Eleanor Maccoby/Carol Jacklin, *The Psychology of Sex Differences* (London: Oxford University Press, 1975); Christine Pierce, "Natural Law Language and Women," in: *Woman in Sexist Society: Studies in Power and Powerlessness*, ed. by Vivian Gornick & Barbara K. Moran (New York: Mentor, 1972).

[9] K. Lewin, *Resolving Social Conflict* (New York: Harper, 1948), chapter 11.

[10] Quoted in Janet White, "On Literacy and Gender", in: *Knowledge about language and the curriculum*, ed. by Ronald Carter (London: Hodder & Stoughton, 1990), p. 181.

the boy who can barely write his own name is excused on the basis of having 'flair', of being 'bored'..."[11] This observation can also be found in contemporary German pre-Pisa empirical studies of teacher-pupil interaction.[12]

Apparently there is no panacea, as Alexandra Frean maintains in *The Times* of July 6, 2007.[13] Employing more male teachers "to act as positive role models"[14] is seen as too simplistic an approach to close the gender gap on learning as the problem is much more complex than that. A report by the new Department for Children, Schools and Families, entitled *Gender and Education: The Evidence on Pupils in England*[15] states that neither adopting more "boy-friendly" methods of teaching nor single-sex schools could provide answers in themselves as the relevant social and psychological undertones have to be taken into consideration, too. "Combatting images of laddish masculinity and a strong school ethos were seen as central to raising the attainment of boys."[16]

In her article, which is based on several studies, Janet White mentions a number of reasons for gender differences in literacy development: the tradition of the genteel, educated female, teachers who (sometimes unconsciously) repeat sex-stereotyped educational practices, and also the reading predilections of children and adolescents, since "children can write only those texts which they know how to read."[17] So the conclusion may be drawn that girls' narrower interest in 'passive' genres of reading and writing puts them at an educational disadvantage in a system which places a premium on spoken skills. "The real positions of power and influence in our society necessitate command of genres for which boys' educational experience provides an appropriate preparation and girls' does not."[18]

As a variation on the more immediate experience of gender and literacy, attention may be drawn to the seeming contradiction that if the statement that girls write better is true, why then is there hardly any female literary tradition worth mentioning? "Jane Austen (see also text 5), for example, worked [...] in a genre that had been dominated by women for a century and one that was looked upon as trash ..."[19] Even as late as 1928 advice was given to female novelists "to acknowledge 'the limitations of their sex' with Austen as the shining example."[20] The background to this lack of esteem for female writing has been well researched, since it was a major issue among feminists in the 1980s.[21]

Awareness

It will be a fascinating undertaking not only to compare reading lists in general, but even more so to compare those of female and male students and to find out to what extent they comply with the statements made in the text about the reading experience of boys and girls (ll. 11 ff.). Moreover, this empirical investigation could also reveal whether students' reading and lending library conventions are in line with what the text says in ll. 14 ff.

The importance of reading bedtime stories to children from an early age, not only as an element of child-parent bonding (see *Students' Book* p. 34), but also as a 'ploy' in promoting literacy has not been disputed. Even the Internet provides bedtime stories that busy parents can download – though this may defeat the purpose, as the ritual of a parent sitting down by a child's bed, book in hand, will no doubt provide a model to be emulated later in life. This model behaviour works on two levels: children who see their parents read books will not consider it unusual to do the same and will also be more likely to read bedtime stories to their own children.

Students could be asked to list their favourite bedtime stories when they were young and could also be motivated to write some themselves (see also *Students' Book*, p. 37, Project 14). They will be in the best of company, as the US-American pop icon Madonna has successfully published six children's books.

The Text

The sexual/gender stereotypes mentioned in the text are also educational stereotypes, which suggest that girls are better at languages and the humanities in general, whereas boys have a reputation for being more successful in maths and natural sciences. From these examples of stereotyping at school it is generally concluded that

---

[11] Janet White, pp. 181f.
[12] Ilse Bremer, Hildegard Küllchen, Lisa Sommer, *Mädchen, Macht (und) Mathe, Geschlechtsspezifische Leistungskurswahl in der reformierten Oberstufe* (Düsseldorf: Parlamentarisches Staatssekretariat für die Gleichstellung von Frau und Mann beim Ministerpräsidenten des Landes NRW, 1989).
[13] Alexandra Frean, 'Male teachers will not close attainment gap, study says', *The Times*, July 6, 2007, p.13
[14] ibid.
[15] www.dfes.gov.uk/rsgateway/DB/RRP/u015238/index.shtml
[16] *The Times*, p.13
[17] Janet White, p. 182.
[18] C. Poynton, *Language and Gender: Making the Difference* (Oxford: OUP, 1989), p. 36.
[19] Joanna Russ, *How to Suppress Women's Writing* (London: The Women's Press, 1984) p. 100.

[20] a.a.O., p. 100.
[21] A publication which covers the question in detail is Nicci Gerrard *Into the Mainstream. How Feminism Has Changed Women's Writing* (London: Pandora, 1989)
Another interesting study, which was seminal, is Sandra M. Gilbert/Susan Gubar, *The Madwoman in the Attic: The Woman Writer and the Nineteenth Century Literary Imagination* (New Haven, Conn.: Yale University Press, 1979).
A recent German publication, entitled *Frauen, die lesen, sind gefährlich*, by Stefan Bollmann deals with the history of reading women portrayed in paintings, drawings and photographs. It covers various eras, countries and motifs and provides an interesting background foil to both the above topic and the related visual material of the reading woman (München: Sandemann, 2005).

certain subjects are marked out for girls (e.g. languages and writing), whereas others are marked out for boys (e.g. maths and natural sciences), and this is often treated like a natural law. This phenomenon indicates that a stereotype operates in such a way as to prevent differentiated thinking about the concept involved and thus – ultimately – prevents necessary change.

The statistics quoted in the text reveal that in early teenage girls read more than boys and prefer different material (fiction and poetry vs. comics and graphic novels). Furthermore there is a shared drop in reading at the age of 18 to 19, after which women pick up again whereas men do not. Even though female students generally do better in subjects of the humanities, their career chances in later life are less since their aspirations tend to be less ambitious than those of young men so that they will end up in low-paid stereotyped jobs for women.

To help children in their achievements of literacy the Labour Government introduced the Literacy Hour as part of the school curriculum to improve literacy standards. In 1999 boys seemed to have stepped up and improved their performance by 14%. The examination may have been boy-friendly, however, due to the choice of material.

Project

In their design of a school of their choice students can be very creative. It may be an anti-authoritarian concept in the tradition of Summerhill.[22] Furthermore it may be a school without the constraints of a required number of participants per course nor the qualifications for 'Zentralabitur'. It would be based on a wide range of students' interests and could also imply project work beyond the boundaries of individual subjects.

In the discussion about which subjects should be taught in single sex and which in co-educational courses the ranges of natural sciences, languages/art and sports would have to be discussed. But students would also have to become aware of the fact where they see the advantages of co-education. For background information go to www.gsa.uk.com. The Girls' Schools Association informs the public about the benefits of going to a girls' school in the following way:

- single-sex schools are at the top of the examination league tables
- girls and boys do not mature at the same time nor at the same speed
- education at girls' schools is geared specifically to their needs
- the girls of today should have no limitations on their professional or personal ambitions to become tomorrow's leaders
- leadership, independence, integrity and an instinct to achieve are necessary for women to juggle their future roles
- girls' schools offer a modern and challenging learning environment in the 21st century
- girls' schools prepare girls for a rapidly changing world
- girls' schools do not just offer equal opportunities but every opportunity
- girls' schools are more likely to provide positive role models for girls.

A radically different view of achievements in co-educational as opposed to single-sex schools is taken by the National Literacy Trust (cf. www.literacytrust.org.uk) which comes to the conclusion that single-sex schools do better only because they get the best pupils (quoting results of researchers at London University's Institute of Education, published in *Independent* and *Express*, 12 August 1999). Further it maintains that "teenagers who attend single-sex schools do no better in exams than those in co-ed schools, according to research from the Institute of Education in London, but they are twice as likely to study subjects not traditionally associated with their gender."

The researchers found that 22% of pupils in all-girls' schools gained maths, chemistry or physics A-levels, nearly twice as many as in co-ed schools. Boys in single-sex schools were similarly more likely to take English and modern language A-levels.

The findings come from a long-term study on the lives of nearly 13,000 people who were teenagers in 1974 and are now in their 40s. The study found pupils in single-sex schools were also more confident in their ability to do well in these subjects and girls were more likely to gain qualifications in male-dominated subjects at university and go on to earn higher salaries.

However, the research, which was funded by the Economic and Social Research Council, shows single-sex education made almost no difference to exam results. Boys do no better once their family background and previous ability were taken into account. Girls did fractionally better at O-level than girls in mixed schools but did no better in further and higher education."
(TES, 22 September 2006)

As this material lends itself to a highly controversial discussion this project can alternatively be turned into a role play entitled "Do we need girls' schools?" for which the role cards on p. 61 may be used. Furthermore it could be used to practise the "art form" of a formal debate.

---

[22] Summerhill, still somewhat controversial today, is a co-educational boarding school in Suffolk, G.B. It was founded by A.S. Neill in 1921 as an alternative 'free' school in the tradition of 'Reformpädagogik'. For background information go to www.summerhillschool.co.uk.

Internet Project 8

What is the National Curriculum for England?
The National Curriculum sets out a clear, full and statutory entitlement to learning for all pupils up to the age of 16. It determines the content of what will be taught and sets attainment targets for learning. It also determines how performance will be assessed and reported. An effective National Curriculum gives teachers, pupils, parents, employers and the wider community a clear and shared understanding of the skills and knowledge that young people will gain at school.

The National Curriculum is regularly reviewed to ensure that it continues to meet the changing needs of pupils and society. This revised National Curriculum principally reflects changes made to the key stage 4 curriculum from 2004. These changes enable schools to offer pupils greater choice, while ensuring they acquire the core of general learning and experience essential to later learning and employment. At key stage 4, young people should see how their studies will lead to further education and employment and be helped to develop competence in skills such as analysis, problem solving, reasoning and communication.

The key stage 4 curriculum should:
- challenge all students whatever their ability
- use curriculum flexibility to motivate students and encourage achievement
- encourage institutions to work together to deliver programmes suitable for each student.

The following are compulsory at key stage 4: English, mathematics, science, ICT, physical education, citizenship, religious education, sex education, careers education and work-related learning. The arts, design and technology, the humanities and modern foreign languages are entitlement areas at key stage 4. This means schools must make available courses in each of these areas to all students who wish to study them.

Work-related learning is a new statutory requirement at key stage 4. This handbook includes a non-statutory framework for work-related learning, which sets out the minimum experience schools should provide. Careers education is now statutory from year 7.

National curriculum online also has information about the changes to the key stage 4 curriculum.

One of the most important strategies the government has developed to raise the level of literacy is the literary hour which is intended to teach children how to read and write on the basis of several activities. One method was, e.g., to invite contemporary authors to teach children and talk with them about literature. www.literacytrust.org.uk advises teachers on how to structure a literary hour for children at primary school level.

The programme is supplemented by even more encompassing approaches such as The National Reading Campaign which is to propagate the joys of reading across all communities, and the Family Reading Campaign (cf. www.familyreading.org.uk) which is to promote reading as a joyful family activity, which may also instigate some aspects of the process of 'bonding'. A definition of 'bonding' can be found in the *Students' Book* on p. 34.

There is a plethora of useful information on 'Boys' reading choices', 'Men, fathers and literacy' or 'Boys, girls and literacy' etc. on the website of the National Literacy Trust.

Internet Project 9

Key skills are defined as "A set of generic skills, which start at level 1 of the qualifications framework, designed to help learners improve their performance in communication, application of number, IT, working with others, improving own learning and performance, and problem-solving." They are also necessary to promote lifelong learning which "describes an individual's capacity to continue to learn and, by implication, to respond positively through learning and development to changing circumstances. Lifelong learning is helped by a capability in ICT so that learning can be undertaken by self-study, remote access and distance learning at times and in places convenient to the learner." (www.qca.org.uk/14–19/toolkit/glossary.htm)

Students might find it an interesting, but also entertaining exercise to test their skills competence by doing manifold exercises with the help of the key skill trainer www.keyskills4u.com. At the same time their linguistic competence will benefit tremendously.

There are some areas in German education which are congruous with the standards applied in British education, e.g. standardised tests for years 8 and 10, but also 'Kernlehrpläne' for major subjects such as German, English, mathematics. Other skills, such as working with others, improving one's own performance or problem-solving are often subsumed in the 'neo-German' generic term "soft skills", which are required in job application procedures and interviews and which students are confronted with, when they are taught how to apply for a job or while doing work experience.

Changing Roles of Women

3 | "The Seneca Falls Convention"

text type: historical pamphlet
length: 915 words
degree of difficulty: ***; 45 annotations and 1 explanation
theme: the first equal rights convention ever and the beginning of the woman's rights movement in the U.S.
teaching points: political register; important documents of U.S. history; discrimination against women in U.S. history

related visual material: two historical posters 'The second class status of women' (U.S.) and 'What a woman may be ...' (GB)

for extra information on 'Noteworthy Dates' see *Students' Book*, p. 15 and Information Sheet: "Historical Development of the Women's Rights Movements in the U.S. and Britain"; for extra information on the wording of the invitation to the Convention see *Students' Book*, p. 11; for additional background material see Information Sheets "Main Tendencies in the Women's Movement" and "Suffragettes on Hunger Strike in Holloway"

The ideas of the women involved in the Seneca Falls Convention were seminal for the development of the Woman's Rights Movement in America. The role of the American Victorian woman was by and large not so different from that in England, but unless students are interested in history they will not know much about either. In order to make the historical context clear it is necessary to draw attention to the radical economic and social changes brought about by the Industrial Revolution, and its noticeable reverberations on the relationships between the sexes. Even before, there had been women rebels, of course, but they had been indviduals without any noteworthy following. The advent of the feminist revolution was foreshadowed by the thought and writing of individual women, members of the contemporary intellectual elites: by Margaret Wollstonecraft and Mary Shelley in England, by Margaret Fuller in America and by the Bluestockings in France. Only by the middle of the nineteenth century, when industrialization was in full swing, was there a real feminist movement.[23] In the U.S. this movement was influenced by the abolitionist struggle, i.e. the struggle for the abolition of slavery, in which many women were involved, and by the ideas of the American Revolution itself. This is why *The Declaration of Sentiments* (1848) was modeled on *The Declaration of Independence* (1776).

What these early feminists were up against was the Victorian cult of true womanhood, which can be characterized by what was considered to be its four main virtues: piety, purity, submission and domesticity. To be a woman was determined by the roles of being a wife and a mother. Female activities outside this realm were unacceptable. The cult of true womanhood evoked the myth of the powerful role of a wife and a mother in her domestic environment. However, the socially sanctioned role of a wife was anything but influential, since married women were legally, economically and emotionally dependent on their husbands.[24]

Awareness

The Declaration of Independence of 4 July 1776 marked the assertion of the idea of complete independence in the 13 American colonies. The British authorities had been unwilling to make concessions to the colonists. In addition to economic dissent over taxation there was territorial and religious disagreement. *The Declaration of Independence*, which contributed to the victory of the American colonies in the War of Independence (1775–1783) and finally to the U.S. becoming an independent country, was a statement of moral principles by which political actions can be evaluated. Its main tenets are that "all men are created equal", that they have "certain inalienable rights, that among these are life, liberty, and the pursuit of happiness", and that governments are instituted to protect these rights. Thomas Jefferson (1743–1826), the author of the *Declaration* and third president of the U.S., expressed the political ideas held by many Americans, but in doing so, he summed up the political doctrine and philosophy of the Enlightenment, especially of John Locke (1632–1704).

The message of the two illustrations is obvious and very similar. In both, women are portrayed as learned academics. In the British illustration five female roles are shown. In addition to academic roles there are those in which women do community service. Men, on the other hand, are portrayed as psychologically, morally or mentally unfit. They do nothing to contribute to the community. In the American poster, the company of those men is to reveal the second class political status of women. In the British poster the message is stated more directly: even though women may hold much more responsible positions in society, they are not allowed to

---

[23] See Shulamith Firestone, "On American Feminism," in: *Woman in Sexist Society: Studies in Power and Powerlessness*, ed. by Vivian Gornick & Barbara K. Moran (New York: Mentor, 1972), pp. 665 ff.

[24] See Elisabeth Kuppler, "Weiblichkeitsmythen zwischen gender, race und class", in: Genus. *Zur Geschlechterdifferenz in den Kulturwissenschaften*, ed. by Hadumod Bußmann & Renate Hof (Stuttgart: Kröner, 1995), pp. 262-287.

The Text

The authors of *The Declaration of Sentiments* see their relationship with men as strained. The detailed list of examples which they provide reveals them as exploited by a patriarchal system. Their intention is to end this tyranny and to assume a state of equality and justice in society. They make the following demands:

(1) We want the right to vote. (2) We want to participate in the formation of laws. (3) We want the same rights as everybody else. (4) We want to be represented and refuse to be oppressed. (5) Even as married women we want to have civil rights. (6) We want to have our own property and money. (7) We want to be morally responsible for our actions, even the bad ones. (8) We want to decide about the cause for divorce and the guardianship of our children. (9) We want to decide about the taxation of our property. (10) We want to have profitable employment and equal pay. We want the same wealth and entitlement to distinction. (11) We want equal education. (12) We want equal positions in the establishments of the Church and the State. (13) We want to be judged by the same code of morals as men. We reject double standards. (14) We want men to give up their unjust God-like position. (15) We want to lead independent, respected lives.

The introduction to these 15 complaints (which will be recognized by all those who are familiar with *The Declaration of Independence*), the complaints themselves as well as the following resolutions are presented in highly formal and intellectually demanding and, at the same time, slightly archaic English, because it is Victorian. Syntactically, it is extremely well-structured (parallelism: ll. 27, 29, 31, 38, 40, 43, 59, 77, 83, 89, 94, 100; ll. 129, 133); lexically, there are allusions to the Bible (ll. 85f., 94 ff., 139), philosophical concepts and laws. The state-philosophical ideas of the enlightenment are obvious (e.g., ll. 1–21, 115–125, 129 ff.). All the arguments put forth are well-balanced and logically irrefutable.

The document contains a plethora of rhetorical devices: e.g., parallel sentence structure, parenthesis, assonance, enumeration, etc. The tone, however, seems completely unemotional, even though the document deals with a highly emotional topic. The register is a mixture of legal and philosophical language.

If one compares the motivations behind the two Declarations, one notices parallel concerns: in both cases there are groups who feel oppressed and legally as well as morally entitled to achieve independence. Even though there is a difference in the oppressor – and thus addressee – the arguments and the linguistic expression given to them are very similar. Women as one half of humankind feel they have been excluded long enough and want to claim their share in those rights that men have adopted exclusively for themselves. To express their claims in the words and the tone of *The Declaration of Independence* is a rather clever means, since no rational human being can deny the justification of the concern.

Even though the text of *The Declaration of Sentiments* is about gender, there are subtexts which refer to race and class. A number of the women involved in the movement did not comply with the ideal of true womanhood personally, because they were not married. But they were, of course, highly educated and frequently of independent means. For them the subtext referring to class meant privileged 'middle class,' and the subtext referring to race meant even more privileged 'white.' But even they could not deny the cultural and ideological soil of 'true womanhood,' in which they had their roots. Any woman not belonging to either of these privileged groups would find it difficult to make their voice heard. The following historical example may help to cast some light on this complex problem. In 1893, for the Chicago World Exhibition, there was a *Board of Lady Managers* involved in the realization of one facet of the American Dream, the optical illusion of the White City. Women organized a Women's Congress, which lasted for a week. But black women were, of course, excluded from the world exhibition and from the *Board of Lady Managers*.[25] Despite the re-interpretations of the 'cult of true womanhood' that white women had made for themselves, there was no room for black women.

Internet Project

Some ideas about Third Wave Feminism which originates in the 1990s:

Third Wave Feminists have sometimes been called 'rebels without a cause', as there does not seem to be a unifying issue to turn their ideas into a 'movement'. Second Wave feminists grew up when the politics were the culture, with such events as "Kennedy, the Vietnam War, civil rights, and women's rights"; while the Third Wave sprung from a culture that included "punk-rock, hip-hop, zines, products, consumerism and the Internet". This is a major difference between second and third wave feminists. Third wave feminists grew up understanding and learning about feminist issues that came to them due to the political culture and activism that is the Second wave.

The following websites might be of interest for researchers into Third Wave Feminism:

Third-wave feminism – Wikipedia, the free encyclopedia

---

[25] See Kuppler, pp. 281f.

The 3rd WWWave propagates feminism for the new millennium of the women who juggle a career, a family, a house, a bank account etc.

4 | William Congreve "Battle of the Sexes"*

text type: (extract from) drama
length: 1140 words
degree of difficulty: ***; 116 annotations and 5 explanations
theme: the conditions of a marriage contract in the 17th century
teaching points: drama; legal aspects of marriage; rhetoric

related visual material: drawing of a scene from a contemporary play

for extra historical information on the Restoration see *Students' Book*, p. 18; for extra information on the contemporary attitudes towards marriage see *Students' Book*, p. 19

The spirit of the period of the Restoration can best be understood, if it is juxtaposed with what preceded it: the Cromwellian Commonwealth, in which 'Lord Protector' Oliver Cromwell and his republican successors exercised the power of government. Psychologically, for the people at that time, the rule of austerity changed into a spirit of *joie de vivre* and, to a certain extent, frivolity. Politically, the Restoration of 1660 restored King, Parliament, and law in place of the forced power of military dictatorship. Ecclesiastically, it restored the Anglican attitude to religion, in place of Puritanism. Socially, the Restoration restored the nobility and the gentry to their hereditary place.[26]

The re-opening of the theatres gave a boost to Restoration drama. The revived theatres differed in several respects from their predecessors. The playhouse was roofed in, the stage artificially lighted with candles, there was a drop curtain and painted scenery. The women's parts were no longer played by boys, but by women actresses. Men came to see the actress as much as the play. Restoration theatre was a new theatre with new possibilities for a new dramatic art – and new dangers. In 1698, Jeremy Collier wrote his famous attack against Restoration theatre and its representatives, entitled *A Short View of the Immorality and Profaneness of the English Stage*.

Players and playwrights were at the mercy of a surprisingly small theatre-going public, a coterie of aristocratic, well-to-do, fashionable people ('the Town'), living for the most part in the western suburbs of London, and closely related to the Court. The respectable London middle classes shunned the theatres, and the lower classes preferred rougher forms of entertainment.

Contemporary English drama and English culture were very much 'upper class'. The Restoration period was particularly self-conscious about those social practices which distinguished it from pre-Commonwealth England, and Restoration comedy provided the main literary outlet for this self-consciousness. The Comedy of Manners evolved in response to these new habits and values. Its common elements were the love duel, the fop, the libertine, the conflict between generations, the contrasts between country and town, between England and France. There was a preoccupation with love, an emphasis on sex-antagonism, the common conventions being that marriage is a bore and love primarily or exclusively a physical appetite.[27]

Awareness

With a rising divorce rate in post-industrial countries there is an ever increasing awareness that marriages do not always last a life-time – "till death do us part". Divorces are expensive. So people look for security in case they have made a mistake. In order to minimize the negative economic consequences of divorce they agree on a marriage contract before they take the marriage vows.

The Text

The text is an excerpt from the famous proviso (a proviso is a necessary condition in an agreement) scene of *The Way of the World*, in which the 'gay couple'[28], the hero Mirabell and the heroine Millamant bargain about the conditions of their future marriage. The proviso scene was 'invented' by John Dryden (1631–1700), who turned the scene in which the hero and heroine bargain about the conditions under which each might contemplate marriage into a successful stereotype of his plays. The bargaining between Mirabell and Millamant, however, has never been surpassed in brilliancy and wit. The proposal of marriage never deteriorates into sentimentality. The negotiated contract is one between equals.[29]

---

[26] G.M. Trevelyan, *English Social History* (Harmondsworth: Penguin, 1980), pp. 267f.

[27] See P.A.W. Collins, "Restoration Comedy", *The Pelican Guide to English Literature. From Dryden to Johnson*, ed. by Boris Ford (Harmondsworth: Penguin, 1966), pp. 156 ff.

[28] In the context of the English Restoration 'gay' does not mean 'homosexual', as it does today, but 'full of mirth', 'light-hearted'.

[29] See Malcolm Kelsall, *Congreve: The Way of the World* (London: Edward Arnold, 1981), pp. 38 ff.

Mirabell has charm and grace which win the heart of all women. He has been a rake and a libertine with a mistress of many years. When he thought that his mistress was pregnant by him, he married her off to another man. Millamant, though having good reason to fear Mirabell, is wooed by him with honest respect and love, and is won by a man who convinces her that he will be a good husband and *not* in the way of the world.

Millamant has charm and good looks, too, and puts up the front of a coquette. Behind it there is a woman of needle-sharp wit. She uses both her attractiveness and her wit to give pain if she thinks it fit. She masks her feelings behind affectation, which results from her vulnerability as a woman, both economically and emotionally. Millamant's financial situation depends upon marrying with her aunt's consent. Thus Millamant must consider the emotional risk of entering into a love relationship and the financial consequences. Mirabell proves highly suitable on both counts.

What the lovers share is the ability to reciprocally catch each other's thought and mood. The scene begins with a quotation from Edmund Waller's (1606–87) poem "The Story of Phoebus and Daphne Applied": "Like Daphne she as lovely and as coy", by which Mirabell completes a couplet begun by Millamant, i.e. "Like Phoebus sung the no less am'rous boy", which are ll. 3 and 4 of the poem. The original classical myth concerns an attempted rape. The tale by Waller has become a praise of the art of perpetual courtship. The mistress maintains her 'cruelty' by always fleeing. This idea is adopted in l. 4, where the word pursuit connotes a chase.

The love relationship that Millamant and Mirabell negotiate about is based on mutual respect, on equal terms and on good breeding. There is an element in the scene which suggests a manual for married etiquette, the writing of which might be a task to set for the students, especially in comparison with a potential modern version. With attention to detail the minutia of married existence are evoked: the regime of the tea-table, make-up, drink, relatives one does not like, the need for privacy. The latter is one important facet in Millamant's concept of liberty, with which she associates personal freedom, even in marriage. Having seen many pathetic examples of marriages, Millamant wants hers to be different.

Lists of conditions:
Millamant:
- wants to get up as late as she pleases,
- no terms of endearment allowed,
- no familiarity in public,
- right to her own private correspondence,
- dines alone, whenever she wants to,
- her husband must not touch her closet,
- she has her own tea-table,
- her husband must knock before entering.

Mirabell:
- wants to get up as early as he pleases,
- his wife must not have a confidante of her own sex,
- nobody is to take her to the theatre in pursuit of fops,
- no false pretence allowed,
- she must be content with the way she looks,
- no exotic or 'weird' cosmetics allowed,
- no fancy trimmings from the traders,
- no corselet, etc. when she is pregnant,
- only non-alcoholic drinks to be served at the tea-table,
- tea-table talk must be the usual gossip.

From the two lists of provisos as well as from other topics they talk about it may be concluded that these aristocratic ladies and gentlemen were people of leisure, with a strong interest in entertaining or being entertained, either by going to the theatre or other public places (like parks) in order to be seen, or by giving parties in their own homes.

There was a belief in the power of all kinds of exotic or 'weird' cosmetics just as there was a strong belief in superstition. Women must have been very vain when they were pregnant, even to the point of endangering the foetus by wearing garments that were too tight. Alcoholic beverages must have been fashionable with women, too. The fashion of the day was based on anything French and also exotic things from the colonies or acquired in foreign trade. Husbands must have felt to be the masters of their wives (opening closets, etc.); married partners must have spied on each other.

A typical day in the life of Mrs Millamant, a lady of leisure, can easily be imagined: she will get up as late as she pleases, have a leisurely breakfast in her room, dawdle, get dressed and then go to Hyde Park in a carriage or go to the theatre with a friend. Later, she will expect her friends for tea at her home, have the most exotic titbits served which are in line with a fashionable tea-table. She will write letters to some private correspondents and talk to her friends.

In addition to cultural clues gathered so far there are more signs to be decoded: the medicinal clues in this excerpt must be read against the background information that the Restoration was both a period of scientific experiment and superstition. This can be seen in the ingredients of cosmetics: hog's bones, hare's gall (l. 100), etc. Since there were no artificial chemicals, natural products had to be used. The therapeutic effect of some of these cosmetics, however, was based purely on superstition.

Since coffee and tea had only recently been introduced to England, tea-tables and coffee-houses were highly fashionable.

Going to the theatre was so important a pastime, because upper-class people of leisure had not much else to do, and because the theatres had been closed at the time of Oliver Cromwell. Women wore vizards and masks either to tease or not to be recognized by their husbands or other people.

Language was different. People used it to prove their wit (or camouflage their lack of it). The language used by contemporaries of the Restoration sounds stilted and flamboyant to the modern ear, because it abounds in rhetorical devices. The purpose of the quotation at the beginning of the scene is not only to show the telepathic relationship between the couple, but also their intellectual standing. The metaphor of the wild goose chase (ll. 2 ff.) is elaborated upon in the equivalent semantic field: search (l. 2), chase (l. 4), pursuit (l. 4), fly (l. 5), follow (l. 6), here also solicit (l. 10). Some French expressions are integrated (ll. 35, 37), which is in accordance with the aristocratic fashions of the time. There are contrasts and paradoxes (e.g. ll. 9f., 66f.), parallel sentence structure, enumerations (e.g. ll. 36f., 46f., 116, 117f., 122 ff.). Alliteration can be found in phrases like "fond, fulsomely familiar, before folks" (ll. 48 ff.). There is a repetition of "positively" (ll. 38, 44) for emphasis, a repetition of imperatives ("let us"; ll. 55 ff.), and a repetition of "item", "imprimis", "article", which – in legal language – are signs of a contract.

The scene follows a climactic movement from the mock pursuit at the very beginning to the agreement about the contract at the very end. Here, the 'battle of the sexes' ends with a reasonable reconciliation, which sets it off positively against the predominantly cynical attitude of Restoration dramatists towards marriage. The positive stance is based on the honesty between the hero and the heroine. Millamant's demands reveal her disillusionment with the behaviour of married partners towards each other: the unavoidable familiarity tempts partners to take liberties with each other or to take each other for granted, which will eventually result in a loss of mutual respect.

From a literary point of view this scene is a classic example of the 'battle of the sexes', as it follows the pattern that sexual antagonism is resolved in marriage. However, from a psychological point of view there is a difference in the sense that Millamant is much stronger and more emancipated than women were in those days.

5 "It is a truth universally acknowledged ...": Jane Austen and the Marriage Market

text type: (extract from) novel
length: 594 words
degree of difficulty: **; 25 annotations
theme: a rejected proposal
teaching points: analysis of novel; verbal and non-verbal behaviour; the marriage market as an apt metaphor of gender role difficulties; the landed gentry in 18th century England

related visual material: two stills from the 2005 film version of *Pride and Prejudice*; a picture of Basildon Park, one of the locations for the 2005 film version

Historical Context

Jane Austen (1775–1817) is among the best-known writers of the 18th century, though she has only written 6 novels, an unfinished fragment and an abundance of letters to various family members, but especially to her favourite niece Fanny and her sister Cassandra. Despite the fact that Jane Austen's life 'saw' the French Revolution, the Napoleonic Wars and the Battle of Waterloo, she has often been considered to be a chronicler of the gentry, as her novels are set in the typical environment of country life in Regency England. The landed gentry of her time belonged to the leisured classes, spent the greater part of their lives on their country estates, and a smaller part in Bath (the city which still claims Jane Austen fame and arranges various Jane Austen events[30]) where the gentry took the water at the Pump Room[31] and attended balls at the Assembly Rooms, or – less frequently – in London. Work or even a fortune made on the basis of work (here: trade) were anathema to its members.

Jane Austen has both been praised and criticised by numerous schools of criticism, praised for what her novels deal with and criticised for what they ostensibly ignore. Her main achievement, however, is her treatment of the roles of women in the society she knows so well, their specific relationships with men and the symbolic meaning of the marriage market. Thus her novels ideally lend themselves to an investigation of gender roles. What

---

[30] If you want to find out about the annual Jane Austen festival go to www.janeaustenfestival.co.uk; if you want to contact the Jane Austen Society in Britain go to www.janeaustensoci.freeuk.com, if you want to contact the German friends of Jane Austen go to www.janeausten.ja.funpic.de, all of which will help you to turn yourself and/or your students into a proper 'Janeite'.

[31] The Pump Room, officially opened in 1795 in its present design, contains the King's Fountain which helped to provide invalids with healthy spa water from a clean pump; it is now a restaurant where you can enjoy your tea, listen to the Pump Room Trio and drink a glass of warm Spa water.

is more, the continual Jane Austen "boom", which can be seen in the number of recent film versions, will help students to understand a historical epoch with its system of norms and values which they might otherwise have considered at best to be strange, but more likely to be obsolete.

The given excerpt from *Pride and Prejudice* deals with Darcy's first proposal of marriage, which is one of the key scenes in the novel. Some detailed contextualisation – partly provided by the plot outline in the textbook – will be necessary. The title of the novel refers to values which can only be understood in a contemporary class context. Darcy, who is a member of the nobility and thus above Elizabeth Bennet's position, takes pride in his status and supposed moral integrity and looks down on most of her family members, not only because of their status, but also because of their behaviour in society. From his point of view Elizabeth cannot but accept an offer of marriage from such an eligible man. Elizabeth, on the other hand, takes pride in her social position, because she considers herself to be a gentlewoman in her own right with impeccable principles and thus way above Darcy's criticism. What she does not see at the beginning of her development is the way her own and her family's reputation suffers owing to the partly frivolous, partly discreditable behaviour of her family. In her prejudiced attitude towards Mr Darcy she has long adopted the public opinion about him which considers him to be arrogant, reserved and excessively proud.

In order to understand the gender reverberations Darcy's proposal and Elizabeth's rejection of it connote the contemporary concept of the marriage market must be explained. "It is a truth universally acknowledged" that young women of the gentry at the time of Jane Austen needed husbands to provide them with means and status, as there was very little opportunity for them to lead a respected life otherwise. The marriage market is not a figment of the Austen imagination, but a well documented phenomenon[32] of an era in which the position of women was not equal to that of men. Eligibility for marriage in a man predominantly depended on economic and social status, whereas in a woman it was supplemented by a number of accomplishments to help her secure, if not improve her social status.

The marriage market of *Pride and Prejudice* comprises the following characters: in the female camp there are 5 eligible daughters of the Bennet family, plus Charlotte Lucas, Miss Bingley, Miss Darcy and Miss de Bourgh; in the male camp numbers are restricted to Mr Bingley, Mr Darcy, Wickham and Collins. This lack of proportion triggers off the fictional marriage market in *Pride and Prejudice*, which is first alluded to in the famous introductory sentence of the novel "It is a truth universally acknowledged, that a single man in possession of a good fortune must be in want of a wife."[33] This rhetoric of generalisation[34] is immediately exposed as an extract of the sum total of all the social expectations an eligible gentleman is confronted with. "However little known the feelings or views of such a man may be on his first entering a neighbourhood, this truth is so well fixed in the minds of the surrounding families, that he is considered as the rightful property of some one or other of their daughters."[35] The term 'property' alerts the reader to the outstanding economic connotations of the marriage market.

Awareness

Picture this: a balmy summer evening; a man and woman beautifully dressed; a restaurant by the seaside; a table for two, elegantly set with candles, roses, a bottle of champagne; violins playing a romantic tune in the background; he is holding her hand, gets on his knee and asks her to marry him and be happy with him forever. Could this be the romantic ambience in which young lovers visualise the important question to be popped?

But why is it he who should be the active partner to verbalise what they both have dreamed of? Couldn't she take the initiative? As more and more couples seem to think of unusual places for the wedding ceremony to take place, couldn't the proposal be in a different setting, too, e.g. in a submarine or on top of a mountain, in a balloon, or...? Would the setting affect the wording in any way? This field of speculations could be integrated into a role play to set the scene for and alert students to the cultural and personal differences of Darcy's first proposal.

The aspect of etiquette would probably not play a great role in this scenario of a modern proposal, whereas its importance must not be underestimated in a similar situation at the time of Jane Austen. Etiquette is based on the collective expectations of what is appropriate behaviour in various social situations. Frequently they are orally transmitted, but of course there are also codified versions, such as the German *Knigge*[36]. In 18th century England there was a tradition of "conduct", "courtesy" or "etiquette" books which originated in the Renaissance and originally dealt with the training of the "courtly person", both male and female. These books

---

[32] If one reads between the lines of contemporary conduct books and books of etiquette one soon notices that the education of a woman includes the practising of a number of 'decorative' qualities, i.e. accomplishments, which will help the lady to gain an advantage over her competitors on the marriage market. For a more detailed analysis of that procedure see Annegret Schrick, *Jane Austen und die weibliche Modellbiographie des 18. Jahrhunderts* (Trier: WVT, 1986)

[33] *Pride and Prejudice* (Harmondsworth: Penguin, 1972), p. 51
[34] cf. Renate Mann, *Jane Austen: Die Rhetorik der Moral* (Bern, Frankfurt a. M.: Lang, 1975)
[35] *Pride and Prejudice*, p. 51
[36] Freiherr Adolph v. Knigge wrote a book entitled "Über den Umgang mit Menschen" which has become a synonym of 'good manners' despite the fact that it is much more a philosophical and sociological book about human relations.

were intended to describe the life and the accepted manners of the day for well-bred ladies and gentlemen. Ideally, their code of appropriate behaviour (manners) was supplemented by an underlying ethical code (morals).

As the example of the gentry at the time of Jane Austen reveals, expectations concerning correct social behaviour can be very rigid, but since they have cultural overtones, they are much more flexible in societies which are multi-ethnic or cosmopolitan. However, in certain circles (probably middle to upper class) and in certain professional/social situations (e.g. a job interview or a business lunch/dinner/a dinner with one's prospective parents-in-law) they are still indispensible. That is why e.g. some people moving from Northern England to south of the Watford Gap – even in our day and age – not only take elocution lessons, but also lessons in social etiquette.

The Text

The ambience in which Darcy's first proposal takes place differs considerably from the imagined scene with one's dream man or woman. Determined by "her unwillingness to see Mr Darcy"[37] Elizabeth pretends to be feeling unwell and has not gone to take tea at Rosings, the house of Darcy's aunt Lady de Bourgh. Elizabeth blames him for being the main reason why the budding relationship between her sister Jane and Darcy's friend Mr Bingley has broken down. So when he arrives to enquire about her health, she is not predisposed to welcome him warmly. Darcy, however, comes to the point almost immediately and makes her an offer of marriage. He pays her some compliments which are summed up by the narrator in the phrases that he ardently admires her (l. 59) and has had long-felt feelings (ll. 62f.) for her. Elizabeth must admit that being loved by such a man is a compliment in itself (l. 73) and she feels flattered. But at the same time he eloquently expresses his reservations about the match, based on the reputation and social status of her family (ll. 66 ff.), which does not make the situation any easier. In fact, Elizabeth's pride is hurt so much that she becomes angry (l. 77) and barely maintains her composure. The episode ends with mutual reproaches (ll. 110 ff.). In the novel the conversation goes on with consistent ice-cold antagonism on Elizabeth's part, which develops into an almost unbearable confrontation making any further communication seemingly impossible. Elizabeth refuses to play the role society in general and Mr Darcy have allocated to her.

The episode is charged with emotion, which becomes obvious from the tone and the choice of words used in the dialogue contributions and in the text passages in which the mode of presentation is that of summary.

Darcy uses words from the emotional register, e.g. 'ardently admire' (l. 59), 'love' (l. 59), 'felt and had long felt for her' (l. 63), 'tenderness' (l. 66), 'inclination' (l. 69), 'attachment' (l. 80). This is juxtaposed by his ample use of the sociological register, e.g. 'pride' (l. 66), 'inferiority' (l. 67), 'degradation' (l. 67), 'family obstacles' (l. 68). But even in his description of his feelings his use of the psychological register shows that he has tried to subdue, 'repress' (l. 58) and 'conquer' (l.81) them. While Darcy seems to see this as a sign of the sincerity of his feelings, Elizabeth's pride is completely shattered and even though she pretends to maintain the outward appearance of etiquette, she rejects him in a manner that is contrary to social conventions at the time.

Whereas Darcy's tone changes from emotional (which can be concluded from his agitated manner, l. 56) to pretended 'apprehension and anxiety' (l. 85) to 'a voice of forced calmness' (l. 109), Elizabeth is 'exasperated' (l. 87) by his confidence that she will accept him. Her tone is cutting and ice-cold, when she refers to the conventions of accepted behaviour, but at the same time shows him the cold shoulder in a most offensive manner. Here politeness ('civility', l. 112) is a mere façade.

Elizabeth's non-verbal behaviour is deceptively passive, when she "stare[s], colour[s], doubt[s], and [is] silent" (l. 61). Darcy has to misinterpret her silence as 'encouragement' (l.62) as it is the prescribed appropriate behaviour of a young woman at the time of a proposal. At first, she even feels the – equally prescribed – appropriate sympathy for the candidate who is about to be rejected (ll. 72–75). Darcy's body language, however, contradicts his words, as it expresses his conviction that he will be accepted (ll. 86f.). This inconsistency, which originates from the social and gender roles Darcy is to play in this situation, and the inherent misunderstanding lead to an escalation which ends in mutual reproaches, contained anger, injured pride and subsequent attempts on both sides to gain at least the semblance of composure.

The result of Darcy's first proposal and Elizabeth's rejection of it seems to be an unbreachable chasm of speechlessness.

Project 11

Society at the time of Jane Austen was hierarchically structured. The top tier was made up by the nobility, then there was the gentry, followed by the people in trade who were sneered upon by the gentry because their standard of living was based on the money they had earned in trade. In the country there were gentlemen farmers and peasants and in the towns their were the poor, who had to scrape a living.

Marriages were arranged on the basis of money and to keep the property within the family. The eldest son would inherit, and so it was necessary for the younger sons to find a career in the army, the navy or the clergy

---

[37] *Pride and Prejudice*, p. 219

or, alternatively, to marry into property. That is why they were restricted in their choice of a marriage partner. Women – unless they belonged to some fortunate families of the nobility – would never inherit and for them the only means of social survival or mobility was to find an appropriately rich husband. A lady marrying a peer took his noble status. But why should a peer marry beneath himself? Partly, no doubt, because the landed gentry was often burdened with legal requirements so that a peer might be as interested in trying to land a rich heiress as she was in trying to land him.

Etiquette was of great importance as it was the background foil to hierarchical structures. It comprised a mixture of decorum and artificial elegance and covered all areas of life, such as table manners, precedence and seniority, forms of address, dancing at balls, a country house visit, etc.[38] The following excerpts are merely examples of a rich background foil of social rituals and their required codes of behaviour.

The dinner party
[It] began, naturally with the selection of guests, [...].

At the appointed hour, generally in the neighbourhood of 7 p.m., [...] the guests arrived, although, after mid-century it was mandatory that one be precisely fifteen minutes late. The guests were then shown into the drawing room. [...]

The servant then announced that dinner was served.

The couples in order of status then proceeded "down" (in the town house [...]) or "in" (in the country house [...]) to the dinner that would follow. Typically, the hostess would have arranged it so that the man of the house took the highest-ranking lady by the arm. [...]

After the dessert the ladies withdrew into the drawing room. [...] The gentlemen would even smoke, something that was never done by a gentleman in the presence of a lady, even with her permission. [...]

Eventually, however, the host would perceive that his guests were becoming to free in their speech and suggest that it was time to join the ladies.

How to address your betters:
Lord – to address an earl, marquis, or viscount; often marquis or earl *of* someplace; e.g. the "earl of Derby", which later became "Lord Derby"

Lady – to a marchioness, countess, viscountess, or baroness; e.g. the "marchioness of Derby" became "Lady Derby"

Sir – to a baronet or knight with his first name; e.g. Sir Thomas Bertram

Lady – to the wife of a baronet or knight; e.g. Sir Thomas Bertram's wife in *Mansfield Park* is referred to as Lady Bertram.[39]

The London season and 'coming out'
[...] after a short Easter holiday [...] the real season began, a dizzying three-month whirlwind of parties, balls and sporting events. [...] Despite all the surface gaiety, these latter gatherings revolved around the deadly serious business of marrying off the young girls of the family to eligible and wealthy young men in what Trollope and others referred to as the "marriage market". [...] In fact, her first season marked a dramatic turning point in the life of a well-bred young girl. Until she was seventeen or eighteen, she was not considered socially alive [...]. Then, overnight, everything changed: she was suddenly expected to wear her hair in an adult fashion, and she "came out", [...]. If the girl did not get herself married within two or three seasons she was considered a failure; at thirty a hopeless, permanent spinster.[40]

Internet Project 13
Imdb.com lists 10 film versions of *Pride and Prejudice*, five of which are in the form of TV mini series: 1952 (UK, 6x30 min., starring Peter Cushing as Darcy!), 1958 (UK, 6x30 min., remake of the 1952 version), 1967 (UK, 6x25 min.), 1980 (UK) und 1995 (UK, 3x100 min.) and 4 cinema films: 1940 (USA, filmscript by Aldous Huxley!), 2003 (USA, set in the present), 2004 (*Bride and Prejudice*, UK/USA, Bollywood-Musical) and 2005 (France/UK).

The oldest film version, made in 1938, is a 55-minute-long English TV film.

It may be interesting to mention that there is a great number of films whose titles are puns on *Pride and Prejudice*, e.g. *Pride and Extreme Prejudice, Snide and Prejudice, Passion and Prejudice, Poultry and Prejudice*, but whose plots are considerably different.

The density and complexity of the original plot of the novel may explain why there are so many film versions in the form of series. The stringency of the plot, however, has not been adopted by all film directors.

The great attraction of the plot for film purposes may result from the attractive outward appearance and disposition of its main characters (esp. Elizabeth, Darcy and Jane), whose roles can be cast by good-looking actors and offer an interesting scope of interpretation even for stars like Sir Laurence Olivier or – recently – Keira Knightley. In addition to that there is the riveting

---

[38] Another great source of information is : Marjorie and C.H.B. Quennell, *A History of Everyday Things in England*, vol. III (London, New York: Batsford, 1961)

[39] Daniel Pool, *What Jane Austen ATE and Charles Dickens KNEW* (New York: 1993), pp. 32 ff.

[40] ibidem; a critical essay on the treatment of this topic in Jane Austen's novels is Lloyd Brown, "The business of marrying and mothering", in: Juliet McMaster (ed.), *Jane Austen's Achievement* (London, 1976)

"emancipatory" story of the protagonist, a young woman of great personality and keen intellect who manages – against all odds – to succeed in her life and win a partner who is a good match in more than one meaning of the word. The action contains many comic elements, social satire and witty dialogues, which entertain the viewer despite their underlying social and personal conflicts. The beautiful setting of English manor houses with period accessories and costumes enable the viewer to be completely immersed in the world of Jane Austen, which may – to a certain extent – be a form of escapism from the conflicts of their "real world".

The recent Jane Austen boom, which started in 1995 with the BBC tv series of *Pride and Prejudice*, has not enjoyed undivided praise. Benedict Nightingale, regular theatre critic in The Times, ironically revealed his state of confusion in a review of Michael Fry's dramatisation of *Emma*, when he confessed, "Jane Austen Industries plc cranks on and on, turning out products that merge in my mind into *Northanger Sensibility*, or *Prejudice Abbey*, or *Pride and Persuasion Park*."[41] He did obviously not suffer from 'Jane Mania', an illness diagnosed in the satirical magazine *Private Eye*.[42] Trying to reveal the secret of Jane Austen's sudden attraction, Elsemarie Maletzke sums up American and British press reviews. While some of the former seem to detect a general revival of virtues and good manners, the latter allocate a role to the author which has more commonly been associated with the Royal Family: to unite the British nation across all class borders.[43]

Internet Project 14

14 a The approach to this project will definitely depend on the choice of the film versions, which in turn will depend on how far students have progressed in the skills of media literacy.

A comparison between any two versions will be a fascinating undertaking, but contrasts between dated and modern examples, local and exotic settings, period and contemporary concepts might be more stimulating and perhaps even provoke controversial discussion. For more advanced students in media literacy it might also be a challenge to investigate into the structural differences between a cinema film and a TV series.

The following versions are available on DVD: the film versions of 2005, 2004 (*Bride and Prejudice*), 2003 und 1940, and also the series of 1996 and 1980. There are still some videos available, too.

14 b As dialogue plays a central role in *Pride and Prejudice* (one of the most significant scenes of the novel is presented in the *Students' Book*) it will be advisable to present students with vocabulary of media literacy which is generally used for camera positions in dialogue scenes; e.g. camera angle, camera movement, close-up, medium close-up, detail shot, full shot, long shot, medium shot, point of view shot, tracking shot, over the shoulder shot, reverse style shot, high angle, zoom etc.

In the 2005 version the dialogue of Darcy's first proposal is rendered outside. Darcy follows Elizabeth into a gazebo in the pouring rain. The setting reflects complete isolation and a disharmony of feelings and attitudes. Furthermore, the pouring rain serves as a visual objective correlative (a definition of this literary device can be found in the *Students' Book*, p. 27).

Another vital element of film genre and style is the soundtrack, in addition to which art direction and costume design are important elements of a period piece. The 2005 film version won Oscar nominations in all three categories.

6 Kate Chopin "The Story of an Hour"

text type: short story (complete)
length: 981 words
degree of difficulty: **; 27 annotations and 1 explanation
theme: a Victorian marital relationship
teaching points: analysis of short story; the concept of the objective correlative; creation of suspense

related visual material: watercolor of woman in an armchair

for extra information on Objective correlative see *Students' Book*, p. 27; on Feminism, p. 28

Background

Kate Chopin was brought up in a largely female household in St. Louis, Missouri, a busy cosmopolitan city with a large Creole community. Fortunately Kate married a man who respected her love of privacy and tolerated her unconventional behavior. Oscar Chopin was a Creole working temporarily in St. Louis, married the twenty-year-old belle and took her to live in his native Louisiana, which was to provide the setting for most of her short stories and her two published novels.

American Creoles, the group into which Kate Chopin was born and later married, are white descendants of early French and Spanish settlers in New Orleans, although it is a term often loosely used to refer to any native of New Orleans. True Creoles were rich, aristocratic and conservative. They inhabited the ***Vieux Carré***, the French quarter of New Orleans. Another group

---

[41] Benedict Nightingale, "Haven't we seen this one before?", *The Times*, 19 July 1996, p. 31
[42] quoted in: Elsemarie Maletzke, "Romanzen gehen meistens schief", *Die Zeit*, 16.Februar 1996, p. 70
[43] ibidem

of importance in Louisiana were the Cajuns, descendants of French colonists who settled in Acadia, Nova Scotia in the seventeenth century. When the British claimed the land, the French left and settled Louisiana (roughly from the Lake Charles region to Baton Rouge), but proudly kept their name and heritage: Cajun.

The Chopins' gracious city life of a fashionable Creole family lasted only a few years. Oscar's business did not prosper and they were forced to return to his family's plantation in the Cane River district, where he died of swamp fever in 1882, leaving his wife with six children to support. After paying off her husband's debts, Kate returned to St. Louis and began to write using as material her memories of New Orleans and of Cane River. For that reason she was considered to be a local-color writer at first – a term she herself never approved of. Instead she wanted to be considered as a writer concerned with what she called "human existence in its subtle, complex, true meaning." Friends believe she had much more to say, but lost courage after the reception (rejection) of her novel *The Awakening* (London: The Women's Press, 1978).[44] The book became a scandal, since it described the sexual desires and infidelities of a married woman. Kate Chopin's heroine shows a concern for self-fulfilment at the expense of her duties to her husband and children. True, the New Woman was much discussed in the 1890s, since the mass slaughter of the Civil War had forced many women, newly widowed or condemned to celibacy, to enter work hitherto regarded as masculine domains, in order to ensure their own survival as well as that of the national economy. Economic independence was one thing, however, sexual autonomy quite another. The American society of the 1890s could accomodate, albeit uncomfortably, the "New Woman's" demands for better education, the right to work and to vote. It would not tolerate her desire for sexual freedom. Sex was one of the duties of married life, for which a woman was rewarded with her husband's economic support, and elevation to his pedestal, from which she proclaimed her chastity and fidelity.[45]

Awareness

It may be surprising to some contemporaries that in countries with rising divorce rates people still get married. They happily take their marriage vows and solemnly accept their marriage partners "for better or worse," but it may well happen that after some time they will sue for divorce. With divorce having become relatively simple, couples facing marriage need not worry that they will be tied down forever, if they feel they have made a mistake. They may not consider, however, the financial ties or emotional traumas a divorce may well result in, especially if custody for mutual children is to be considered.

In sociological texts marriage is described as "'a bundle of rights' and as an institution which serves different functions: it establishes legal rights between spouses and the legitimacy of their children, it establishes a domestic group and it links different social groups through relations of affinity. The ceremony of marriage is a rite of passage, marking the change in social status."[46]

In addition to the above-mentioned reasons for marriage one can imagine the following:
- emotional and financial security,
- love,
- combining/complementing family property and assets,
- having a partner for 'life',
- bringing up children in a socially sanctioned environment,
- religious reasons: the family as a sanctioned social unit,
- procreation (no sex before marriage).

Even though an increasing number of women are not dependent on a marriage partner to give them financial security nowadays, it may well be the case that women give up their job to have children, so there may well be a temporary necessity for that enhanced security. What is more, single-parent families are still no socially sanctioned alternative to the nuclear family.

The Text

"The Story of an Hour" is about an hour that changes a person's life dramatically. It is possible to experience something similar, e.g. love at first sight, an unexpected encounter, an accident, a sudden death, but even an insight into the solution of some problem someone may have had; all of these could change a person's life within minutes. One might argue, however, that most events of importance take time to develop in order to result in something fruitful. The outcome of a lot of events can be predicted or even planned and are not as dramatic as the incidents which make up the plot of the short story.

"The Story of an Hour" deals with a wife's unexpected reactions to the news of her husband's sudden death in a railway accident. Her feelings are only revealed to the reader, who is given access to the 'widow's' psyche, and not to the people around her, who think that she has gone into mourning. When Louise locks herself into her room, after weeping in her sister's arms, she behaves like one would expect a mourner to behave, overcome by grief. In her room, however, the 'widow' is overcome by

---

[44] *The Awakening* was first published in America by the avant-garde publishers Herbert S. Stone and Co. on 22 April 1899, and copies were distributed in England in July of the same year.
The introduction to *The Awakening* in the above-mentioned Women's Press edition (pp. vii–xxi) is a well of biographical information on Kate Chopin.

[45] See introduction to the Women's Press edition of *The Awakening*, pp. xii, xv ff.

[46] *The Fontana Dictionary of Modern Thought* (London: Fontana, 1988), p. 503

feelings of freedom and independence, coupled with joy. She anticipates a long life, spent according to her own wishes and plans.

True to its title, "The Story of an Hour" roughly covers the timespan of an hour in the life of Louise Mallard, whose life changes radically, but surprisingly not in the way she anticipates her newly won freedom. In a brainstorming session in her room, she breathes a prayer that her life may be long (ll. 94f.) and looks forward to re-structuring it, but at the end of her train of thought, after she has left her room "like a goddess of Victory" (ll. 98f.), there is an unexpected dramatic twist: her prayer remains unheard, for when Brently Mallard returns, safe and sound, Louise dies instantly of shock. To sum up, one can say that the most dramatic hour in the life of Louise Mallard begins with a falsely reported death, after which the feelings of the supposed widow are elaborated on, and it ends with the protagonist's (real) death, the cause of which is diagnosed as "joy that kills," or in medical terms: "heart disease" (l. 111).

Louise Mallard is a young wife in Victorian America with all its repressive conventions. She has got "a fair, calm face, whose lines bespoke repression and even a certain strength" (ll. 37f.). The use of the emphasizer "even" is an indicator that this strength is not normally to be expected, and one might add, especially in a woman, but Louise proves to be strong in her process of liberation. Her strength overpowers her grief as a mourner.

As she has not got a strong heart, the news of her husband's death must be broken exceedingly gently to her (ll. 1–5). Louise is genuinely shocked, which can be concluded from her weeping with "wild abandonment" (ll. 15f.) and from her passing through "a storm of grief" (l. 16). Only after locking herself into her room, and gradually allowing her deeper feelings to surge up, does she realize that her grief is dominated by more powerful emotions. It is symptomatic, however, that she does not have the courage to face them at first, in fact, she even tries to repress them (ll. 51f.). There is an interior struggle between what she thinks appropriate to a widow, and what she must confront herself with (ll. 43–56). Her real feelings are revealed in an outburst with a very liberating effect. Her facial expressions and psychosomatic reactions are indicative of the dramatic changes within her: a "vacant stare" (ll. 56f.) is followed by "a look of terror" (l. 57), which in turn is followed by "keen and bright" eyes (l. 58), with "her pulses [beating] fast" (ll. 58f.) and her "coursing blood [warming] and [relaxing] every inch of her body" (ll. 59f.). In her anticipation of her liberated future, she visualizes herself as living for nobody but herself. She rejoices at her freedom of "body and soul" (l. 84).

From the above-mentioned description one must conclude that Louise's marriage must have had its flaws, even though they are not stated *expressis verbis*, and even though she admits to herself that she has (sometimes) loved her husband (l. 79). But the lines on her face must have been brought about by her husband's imposition of his will on hers, which in Mrs Mallard's consideration is a common feature of the power struggle between men and women (ll. 74 ff.). She clearly considers the bending of a strong will by an even stronger will "a crime" (ll. 77f.), irrespective of the intention behind it. As a summary one can say that Mrs Mallard has led the perfectly normal, conventional, even comfortable life of a married woman without making it clear to herself that she has felt repressed by her husband. This façade only breaks down when she is falsely informed about her husband's death. This transposition into the state of a mourner gives her the courage to admit her feelings to herself.

This process of self-recognition is described in such a way that the reader is spell-bound. From the very beginning of the story suspense is evoked, first when Mrs Mallard's heart condition is mentioned, second when it is 'confirmed' that Mr Mallard is one of the casualties in a railroad disaster (ll. 8f.). From this point onwards there is a consistent line to be followed: Louise locks herself into her room, which could be interpreted as a sign of her being inconsolable. She sinks into her armchair, which is an expression of her physical exhaustion. Body and soul are mentioned twice, first in the context of her exhaustion (ll. 20 ff.), and later in the context of her new freedom (l. 84). It seems that the tension she experiences at first is resolved in her newly gained freedom. In a similar manner, the author refers to abandonment. First Louise weeps "with sudden, wild abandonment" (ll. 15f.), later she abandons herself to the idea of freedom (ll. 54f.). All of these conflicting emotions are linguistically rendered by means of powerful adverbs and adjectives in collocation with emotive nouns, e.g. "sudden, wild abandonment" (ll. 15f.), "fearfully" (l. 44), "subtle" (l. 45), "elusive" (l. 46), "monstrous joy" (l. 61), "exalted perception" (l. 62), "powerful will", "blind persistence" (l. 73), "feverish triumph" (l. 97), "unwittingly" (l. 98). Suspense is also created by means of comparisons, similes and metaphors, e.g. the comparison between Louise's reaction to bad news and that of other women (ll. 13 ff.); Louise's sobbing is compared with that of a child (ll. 35f.). Something menacing is creeping out of the sky and she is trying to fight back this doom. She carries herself "like a goddess of Victory" (ll. 98f.), but this is only an unreliable, transitory experience, which can be concluded from the description of her triumph as "feverish" (l. 97). Suspense is created, when Louise's sister Josephine kneels in front of Louise's door and communicates through the keyhole (ll. 85f.), and finally when Brently Mallard returns unharmed and Richards tries to shield him from Louise's vision, accompanied by Josephine's piercing cry (ll. 103–108).

One of the most powerful means, however, by which suspense is created is undoubtedly the description of nature through Louise's bedroom window. In literature, the description of nature has frequently been employed to cast a light on very powerful feelings. (Ernest Hemingway is considered to be a master of this technique.) The technical term for this device is 'objective correlative' (see additional information p. 27 of the *Students' Book*). It comes as a surprise to the reader that the description of nature, as it is observed by Louise, is rendered in very positive terms: "aquiver with the new spring life" (ll. 24f.), "delicious breath of rain" (l. 25), "distant song" (l. 27), "countless sparrows were twittering" (l. 28), "patches of blue sky" (l. 30), "drinking in a very elixir of life" (l. 91). This description appeals to the visual, auditory, and gustatory senses. Everything is bustling with new life. If one employs the concept of nature as an objective correlative, this pastiche can only have very positive connotations: it is a very optimistic presentation of a renewed spring, which means a renewal of life for Mrs Mallard.

The structure of the story reveals, however, that this dream is not fulfilled. The story is based on a circular structure, with a tumultuous movement between its beginning and its ending: when the sad news is imparted, the place of action is downstairs in the Mallards' house. In passing, her heart trouble is mentioned. Soon, Louise locks herself into her room upstairs and experiences dramatic changes of a new beginning. On her sister's request she returns downstairs, with only a feverish triumph in her eyes giving away her powerful feelings. Then a key is heard in the lock, and Brently Mallard returns unharmed. The story begins not only where it began, but also in a similar manner, i.e. with a death, but paradoxically the victim is the protagonist, who has just wished for a long life. Fate has turned the tables.

What remains unresolved to the reader are Louise's ambivalent reaction to her husband's death, and her contradictory feelings, especially as she claims to have loved him (sometimes). The reader can only conclude that her relationship with her husband must have been ambivalent, too. She must have experienced her admittedly kind husband, who "had never looked save with love upon her" (ll. 65f.) as a repressor. The conventional aspects of her marriage must have meant a golden cage to her, limiting her freedom and restricting her desire for self-assertion. The dormant conflict within her, which she does not admit even to herself lightly, can only be resolved in self-recognition after her husband's supposed death.

If Kate Chopin was influenced by the leading lights of the Seneca Falls Convention (some of whom she knew personally), then her description of Louise Mallard's process of self-liberation could be seen as a possible result. In all her ambivalence towards her husband and her marriage Louise Mallard may very well represent the typical middle-class wife of her times, who marries someone (she sometimes loves) because it is the accepted form of behavior, and who later realizes that her marriage imposes more than one restriction upon her, which leads to her intense dissatisfaction and possibly brings on her heart trouble.

If Louise Mallard had been invited to the Seneca Falls Convention, she would most probably have gone, in which case she would have signed all three resolutions mentioned at the end of text 3. What her specific complaints would have been can only be speculated on, but it is necessary speculation in view of Project 20.

Project 19

Suggestion for the re-writing of the passage ll. 30–39 from the point of view of a true mourner:

The open square before her house lay hidden in the evening mist so that the tops of the trees were barely visible against the evening sky. They formed gloomy shadows against a darkening background. No sounds were to be heard in the streets below. Nature was preparing itself for yet another winter. A heavy rain had fallen and drenched everything. The oppressive breath of rain was still in the air. Night was imminent. Even the black crows were sheltering somewhere. Mountains of black clouds had piled above one another facing her window. She stood to draw in the evening air and shivered: winter was near.

Changing Roles of Men

7 | William Brandon "The Wild Freedom of the Mountain Men"

text type: expository text (extract from travel writing)
length: 757 words
degree of difficulty: **; 47 annotations and 7 explanations
theme: the 'lone wolf' travelling alone and coping with danger
teaching points: the myth of masculinity; concepts of freedom

related visual material: photo of lone cowboy on a horse (inlay); mountain man with his dog (photo)

for extra information on the mountain men see *Students' Book*, pp. 31f.; for extra information on myth see *Students' Book*, p. 31

Background

What has masculinity got to do with freedom? Is there a link or is it simply a myth, which is propagated in advertisements and T.V. spots? If masculinity refers to the qualities suitable to a man, we must ask ourselves which qualities are indeed suitable to a man. Moreover, what have those qualities got to do with freedom, and why – in the title of the text – is this freedom considered to be wild? There are a number of contradictions, which can be pointed out, but which are most probably irreconcilable.

In the context of the travelogue the picture of the mountain man and his important role in opening up and pushing forward the frontier are presented. Michael Brandon outlines John Charles Frémont's fourth expedition to the West in 1848, which was carried out to survey a railroad route to the Pacific Ocean. For those who participated in it, it was an extreme situation, which took them to the limits of their stamina. These men were glorified as representatives of the early ideal of masculine values and virtues. In this context the concept of the American Crusoe is closely linked to the idea of the American West. Crusoe and the American settlers share a "split consciousness," which results from the contradictions between the experiences of their past and their present realities. Like Crusoe, the American settlers and the Mountain Men had to learn to survive by "reading" nature, a semiotic process of the most basic kind, which ultimately enabled them to control their immediate environment.

"To probe the origins of the American Crusoe one needs only to turn the pages of our national literature. We see him in Bradford's *History of the Plymouth Plantation*, where the Puritan is poised to take from the land what it can give and to use the natives to complete that desire. [...] At the deeper levels of national consciousness, the American Crusoe reflects a value system in which the brightest ideals compete with the most expedient, pragmatic, utilitarian motives. [...] James Fenimore Cooper brought these mixed motives to his Natty Bumppo stories, showing another Crusoe crossing the country from upstate New York to the western prairie. As Natty goes west he leaves civilization behind."[47] Many more literary examples of this American archetype are given in Lehan's essay to outline the contradictions in detail and to investigate into attempts at their reconciliation in American literature throughout the ages.

Awareness

A brainstorming session would possibly bring forth the following ideas, which would then have to be contextualised:

---

[47] Richard Lehan, "Literature and Values: The American Crusoe and the Idea of the West," in: *Making America. The Society and Culture of the United States*, ed. by Luther S. Luedtke (Washington: United States Information Agency, 1992), pp. 178f.

- freedom is the state of being allowed to do or say what you want, freedom of speech, freedom of the press, religious freedom, political freedom,
- abolition of slavery gave the slaves their freedom, absence of bondage, emancipation,
- see also liberty: freedom from a master, too powerful a government or foreign rule,
- when prisoners are released they gain their freedom,
- freedom from hunger or starvation,
- freedom is just another word for nothing left to lose (Janis Joplin),
- freedom fighters are people who try to overthrow their government,
- etc.

This first step in the process of becoming familiar with the text could also result in a mind map. It ought to be left to the choice of the individual teacher to supplement this brainstorming session with philosophical concepts of freedom.

Freedom in the simple notion of individual liberty and unrestraint goes back to the ideas of the French philosopher and political theorist Jean Jacques Rousseau (1712–1778), who in 1750 chose primitive man, the noble savage dancing in the forest primeval as his example of individual freedom. The free trapper in the Rocky Mountains brought Rousseau's dream remarkably to life in western America about half a century later.

The Text

The mountain man leads a hard, lonely and self-reliant life in the wilderness, but is described as "the first inhabitant of America to find himself at ease with the familiar concept of great land distances" (ll. 3f.), which is probably due to the fact that he is following his own interest as a trapper and a hunter. His tools and weapons being very simple and unrefined, the mountain man is able to turn his hand to any necessary task. His only social contacts are "small, loosely organized groups" (ll. 18f.), with whom he travels, and an Indian girlfriend. In addition to that he meets traders and other trappers once a year, which regularly results in a drinking binge.

His life is always endangered by the uncertainties of the wilderness, which mean a constant challenge and make it necessary for him to develop and practice forms of existence and skills of survival. He lives up to his limits, exposed to the elements, and on the move most of the time, the only exception being the intervals he spends in the company of "his" Indian girl, who cares for him.

Even though the mountain man's world is described as "neolithic" (l. 15), which could be seen as an archaic niche in the "Steel Age civilization" (l. 16), from which he originates, his characterization by the author is predominantly positive. This can be proved by the author's choice of words: some of the epithets employed belong to the category one would use for a hero (e.g., "defiantly independent" [l. 12], "individual" [l. 12], "free" [l. 13], "sensual animal pleasure" [l. 21], "glowing eyes" [ll. 22f.]).

Even most of the characterization of the professional group as a whole is highly positive as well: e.g., the description of their atavistic instincts in the hunting episode, their glowing eyes, when they spill the blood, all of these details assume a primitive and slightly savage quality, but with positive connotations. Some similes and metaphors are employed to support this impression: e.g., fighting, hiding, running like agile beasts (ll. 41f.), interlopers with no support to back them up (l. 49). The extended comparison (ll. 39–52) between the lives of the mountain men and those of the Indians results in a more positive depiction of the former. Finally, the national importance of the mountain men, summed up in the metaphor "a vector of force" (l. 65), which is evaluated as an accidental by-product of their activities, is given positive connotations, too.

The only implied criticism can be found in the opinion of those outsiders "sheltered by a civilized world" (l. 62), who are appalled, and in the repeated reference to the distance between the world of the mountain men and the civilized world: "neolithic world" (l. 15) v. "Steel Age civilization" (l. 16), "so far in time and space from the established society" (ll. 50f.), all of which could also imply that they are the last 'dinosaurs', subject to extinction, which is also alluded to, when the author mentions their "brief time" (l. 63).

The freedom of the mountain men is seen as "boundless," (l. 61), of unimaginable dimensions, which are highly individualistic at the same time, and can only be estimated in contrast to "the confines of civilization" (ll. 54 ff.). The concept of freedom described in the text runs parallel to Rousseau's concept of the noble savage dancing in the primeval forest, uninhibited by the constraints of a civilized society. At the same time, Rousseau's ideas are seen as an exalted philosophical concept, whereas the freedom of the mountain men is the materialization of this concept in unlimited space, but limited time, which is given to them as the reward for their efforts. The mountain men are "the freedom fantasy made flesh" (l. 78). The repeated classification of Rousseau's philosophical ideas as "a fantasy" (l. 70, l. 78) is proof of its mythical element. In order to brush up students' knowledge on "myth" make use of the information on p. 31 of the *Students' Book*.

To round off this idea of myth-making, students could be provided with advertisements, in which the myth of freedom and masculinity is used as a structural element, e.g., cigarette advertisements showing lone cowboys in the Wild West, especially Monument Valley. This would be the mountain men projected into the 20th century.

From what has been said so far it has become apparent that the world of the mountain men is a man's world. Women do not occur in this scenario with the exception of the Indian girl, mentioned in l. 25. But she is "owned" by her mountain man like his other possessions. Moreover, she plays the quintessential role of the caring woman, who looks after him, tends to his wounds, and makes a home for him, as much as is possible in the wilderness. This is all the space she is granted in his life; more would probably curtail his personal freedom.

The realization of the concept of freedom exemplified in the way of life of the mountain men is obviously restricted to the vast geographical expanses in the Wild West and is unimaginable in an urban area with high population density. In fact, the two seem to be mutually exclusive, because every individual would soon reach the borderline of his/her own space and touch that of his/her neighbor. This would either bring about conflict or would result in compromise at the expense of one's individual boundless freedom. This is why the project work of writing an assessment of the future life of the mountain men, after the closing of the frontier, is an interesting task. Presumably students will say that the mountain men must have experienced some kind of culture shock, which must have traumatized the psychologically less stable (see background information on pp. 31f. of the *Students' Book*). Some of them will probably have ended as human wrecks.

Whether students will or will not classify the mountain men as heroes, will of course depend on their concept of what a hero is and does, whether a hero is seen as someone who has done something brave or whether a hero is seen as a role model to be emulated. The latter most probably does not fit into modern students' ways of thinking, the former is debatable.

8 | Joolz "Mammy's Boy"

text type: song
length: 276 words
degree of difficulty: *; 11 annotations
theme: mother-son relationship
teaching points: structure of a song; tone in which it is presented; men as sons

related visual material: cartoon showing mother and grown-up son

for additional background material see Information Sheet 2: Katharine Whitehorn, "What Little Girls Are Really Made of"; for role cards for Project 12 see Info Sheet 9

Joolz / dʒuːlz / has become known to a larger audience since she started performing together with the bands *New Model Army* and *Red Sky Coven*. "Mammy's Boy" is not a song in the usual sense of the word, but more in the tradition of *sprechgesang*. This concept is very much in line with the oral tradition of story-telling. Indeed, story-telling is what Joolz most frequently does, even in her poetry. In "Mammy's Boy" she tells the story of a mother-son relationship, which has failed dramatically. The reasons for this can only be speculated on.

Awareness

Parental care and parental feelings are phenomena with which students are familiar, because they have been exposed to them for a life-time. Biologically speaking, parents invest in their children by feeding them, bringing them up and loving them, frequently at the parents' own expense or sometimes at the expense of other children. Is parental love unlimited? Is blood thicker than water? Is it possible for a child to be a mass murderer or a terrorist and the parents to go on loving her/him? Examples of this are well-known. Parents of terrorists have made public appeals, parents of murderers have been interviewed, too. Students ought to discuss this complex situation from their own point of view and apply their own (speculative) value system.

Speculation about the parental role students would like to play in the future will probably depend on what they have experienced so far. If they accept their parents' roles, they will presumably wish to continue in a similar vein. Alternatively, they might wish to counter-react. One interesting question that would lead over to the text is whether parents can do too much. When does parental love become stifling? When are parents possessive? When are they over-protective? In this context it might be a good idea to draw students' attention to the title of one of Joolz' poetry anthologies, *Emotional Terrorism* (Newcastle upon Tyne: Bloodaxe Books, 1990). When does parental care turn into 'emotional terrorism'?

The Text

One fascinating phenomenon of this song is that there are a number of open questions, which cannot be answered beyond doubt, but can only be theorized about. According to the way one reads the signs in the text, one will develop a consistent interpretation. The one element one need not speculate about, however, is that the speaker is a mother who has just been told that her son is a triple murderer. The conversation between the speaker and her interlocutors could take place on the mother's doorstep, in court, or even in a mental home. In the latter case she would be repeating the same conversation to herself again and again, which would be a sign of severe neurosis.

The speaker seems to be a strong woman with fixed ideas, who has been hurt badly. She does not believe in the myth that women are the weaker sex (l. 17), because she believes that men can easily be manipulated by women (l. 19), and will eventually do what their women want them to do (l. 34). Women can seduce them without much effort (ll. 20–23). The speaker claims to have looked through this "technique" quite clearly (l. 12). So, incidentally, have other women (l. 13).

In the speaker's view, men are pitiable clowns, who are interested in their buddies, in matey activities like drinking and watching football, but flatter themselves that they are tough (ll. 30–32). And, what is more, they are completely ignorant of women's tactics (l. 35). Women do not marry because they are in love, but because they want a home of their own and a child to look after and to give their love to (l. 25, l. 29).

The predominant tone employed by the speaker is one of anger and defiance. It is evoked by furious expressions like "D'you think I give a damn?" (l. 4), "I couldn't care less" (l. 41), "Damned solemn faces" (l. 38) – which even assumes a stance of anarchy in the context in which it is spoken, for, after all, she is referring to the sovereignty of the state and its representatives. Her loathing of men is expressed in the phrase "pathetic clowns" (l. 30). A tone of possessiveness is achieved by her use of possessives such as "my son", "my boy" (l. 1), "my own flesh and blood" (l. 2), "my baby" (l. 37), "my child" (l. 42). She sees herself amongst a group of other lasses, who have experienced the same with men, and there is a transitory tone of solidarity.

In the middle part of the song the speaker imitates a tone of seductiveness (ll. 20–23) to show how easily men can be manipulated without even noticing it.

There is also a shade of loneliness and despair in "He's all I've ever cared about" (l. 7), "He's been my world" (l. 9), and even though she ferociously clings to the past, her world is now shattered.

The structure of the song is circular, which is in line with the speaker's train of thought: in the first stanza she starts off with her idea of the feelings of a mother and what her focus in life is. She also expresses her defiance of the law. In the second stanza she expresses her disillusionment and reveals the manipulative tactics of women. She voices her contempt of men, whom she all puts into the same category; she even includes her interlocutors, who are most probably policemen. What she does not or does not want to realize is that her son belongs to that despicable category of human beings, too. In the last stanza, it is revealed that her son is a triple murderer, but she adopts her tone of defiance and possessiveness again. So, despite the shocking news, it is a return to the beginning.

Among the open questions are those concerning the age of the son and the reason for the triple murder. It seems to be fairly certain from the context, however, that the son must be a late teenager or an adult so that the mother's exclamations of "my baby" and "my child" seem completely out of date, but rather reveal that she has lost all her sense of reality. She seems to be a kind of inverted Peter Pan, who does not want her son to grow up. She has missed the moment when it is time for parents to let their children go their own way, the reason being that her son has been her life and has substituted all other relationships.

The son, on the other hand, could have killed the three men in self-defence or he could have run riot. He could be a cold-blooded murderer, who killed with premeditation or it could have been an accident. Alternatively, the deed could be a cry for help, because the son wants to free himself from his dominating mother. A strong mother-son relationship may have its positive points, but it is probably more detrimental than beneficial in the long run. In view of the title of the song, one can imagine that the son has always been made fun of, by his mates and friends, and that in later years he may have found it difficult to enter into an adult relationship with a partner.

Speculations about the reasons for the triple murder immediately lead into the vast field of psychology and Freudian psycho-analysis. This does not mean, of course, that perfection is expected in the role-play involving the court psychiatrist. It is also possible to have the mother talk to a social worker, or even a neighbour. It is much more important to think of possible motivations for the behaviour of the mother and the son, and why the latter escalated in the triple murder. Here as well as in any other role play ultra-realism is to be avoided. (See Information Sheet 9.)

For further information about Joolz and letters to be sent to comment on her poetry or ask questions about it, use the following mailing address:
Joolz Info Service
P.O. Box 162
Bradford BD3 8YH
UK

The Cartoon

The cartoon entitled "Mother's Eternal Presence" shows a grown-up son, with a briefcase under his arm, probably going off to work with his mother following him, flying like a guardian angel and protecting him from harm.

9 | Peter Redgrove "Early Morning Feed"

text type: poem
length: 186 words
degree of difficulty: *; 21 annotations
theme: father-son relationship
teaching points: characteristic elements of poetry, imagery; evocation of feelings

related visual material: photo of baby in a cot

There seems to be a heated preoccupation with the mother-son-relationship, in the course of which one tends to forget the importance of the father-son-relationship. Especially in the New Masculinity Movement this is a major concern. The poem "Early Morning Feed" deals with a father who is obviously very worried about his son, even though the reader does not know the reason. It seems that the son has respiratory problems and the father is on the alert almost all of the time.

Awareness

Not only over-protective parents get into a panic when they think that one of their children is in real – or imagined – danger. Parents may be frightened that their young baby will suddenly stop breathing in the middle of the night and die of the mysterious Sudden Infant Death Syndrome, or 'cot death' in colloquial English. The causes of this death are not entirely clear, even though one knows that there are certain groups of babies at risk (e.g., premature babies and those who are underweight). It must be a tragedy for parents to lose a young baby without any warning. They must be shocked, grief-stricken, and distressed, and will probably think that their mourning will never end.

The Text

The father, whose reactions are described in the poem, concentrates on his son and listens to his son's breathing very attentively. The father's fear and panic are the predominant feelings presented to the reader. There must be some mysterious danger to motivate them. In the poem these reactions are evoked by the father's movements and the alternating speed with which he carries out his movements: sometimes fast ("darts" [l. 1], "gallop" [l.15]), sometimes halting ("on tiptoe" [l. 6], "stands hearkening" [l. 20]). The father keeps listening to the baby's pitch of voice, trying to detect any tone of distress, and the strain of this process is rendered perfectly clear to the reader. It seems as if the baby has just been fed (see: title) and is digesting, which is a difficult time, particularly since the baby seems to be underweight ("light as a violin", l. 16). All the sounds which are reflected in the poem are hushed up, made in the distance, unclear, diffuse, all of which adds to suspense created in the poem, but the father and the reader are fully aware of the fact that this may change any second and that this interval may be just a pause before another panic. This becomes very obvious in the ending of the poem, where the father feels like a wild animal, hiding, but on the alert to keep danger and death away.

The structure of the poem is circular, which implies a return to the beginning. At the beginning of the poem, "the father darts out on the stairs" and finally, "he returns to bed", but the degree of alarm has not diminished. The distance between those two actions is covered by varying levels of suspense and an upward and downward movement (the movement up and down the stairs mirrors the increase and decrease of panic and suspense).

Texts 8 and 9 both deal with parent-child relationships and a comparison between the two is therefore indispensable. The father in text 9 worries about his son, and is protective, but not overprotective (ll. 9f.), whereas the mother in text 8 is possessive and clings to her son far too closely. The son in the poem is only a baby, who obviously has some health problems, so he needs a lot of attention and protection. The son in the song is a grown-up, who has surpassed the level of protection and affection that his mother considers necessary. The mother must have been dominating her son all his life without becoming aware of the fact that she has done him more harm than good. Metaphorically speaking, she has never severed the umbilical cord. The father, however, is conscious of the fact that even at his son's young age there is some power play between the two. This explains the father's hesitation about "springing to his beck and call" (ll. 9f.).

Infant "tyranny" seems an experience that all parents go through at some point: even babies know quite well how to manipulate their parents. In this particular example the father wants to be there in a crisis, but he does not want to be taken advantage of. He finds himself in a conflict that is almost irreconcilable. From his genuine concern about his son's well-being one must conclude that there must be some medical deficiency to justify his behaviour. This implies that the father is not over-protective.

One of the interesting points about this poem is that there is no mother mentioned, even though the son is still a baby. It is a revelation of the reader's own role expectations, if he/she misses the mother in text 9 more than the father in text 8. It is common practice that a young baby should also be looked after by a mother. At this crucial point the reader can find out more about himself/herself than about the whereabouts of the mother, who may be upstairs in bed, sleeping after a night of worries. Alternatively, the father may be the representative of a one-parent family, because he is a widower or divorcee. The father may recently have won custody over the child, not yet knowing how to deal with a young baby.

Legally, unmarried fathers have been at a disadvantage. Sometimes their right to see their children has been curtailed by jealous mothers or even some elderly relatives. With rising divorce rates, too, the question of custody has been pushed into the foreground. It is the task of divorce courts to award custody and a lot of divorced men feel that it is usually mothers who are granted custody. Therefore a number of male pressure groups have been founded, a lot of them claiming that paternal rights have been eroded and that even after a marriage break-up – for whatever reason – joint custody is best for the children concerned. Fathers increasingly refuse to be the providers of money only. In addition to the purpose of fighting for custody, another motivation behind male activist groups is to assert themselves in a new form of masculinity. Men's groups are often a reaction to women's groups, and men's liberation is seen by them as an answer to women's liberation.[48] These ideas are enlarged upon in the context of text 15.

Internet Project

The website gives good advice to fathers, e.g. on how to spend time with their children doing 'bonding' activities, the financial implications of a larger family, helping kids to get over their 'back to school blues' after the summer holidays, but also contains stories from fathers who have recently learned to care for their children.

10 | "The myth of Super Dad"

text type: newspaper article (feature story)
length: 1041 words
degree of difficulty: **; 36 annotations, 11 explanations
theme: a tongue-in-cheek account of New Labour's attempt at promoting new fatherhood; different types of male gender roles

related visual material: a photo of Tony Blair with his baby son Leo; a cartoon serving as a humorous view on paid paternity leave

additional material: an info box on bonding at the end of text 8, p. 34

---

[48] An interesting book, which shows various aspects of the male attitude, is Lynne Segal, *Slow Motion: Changing Masculinities, Changing Men* (London: Virago, 1990).

"The myth of Super Dad" | Gender Roles – Resource Book

Biography of Tony Blair

Tony Charles Lynton Blair was born on May 6, 1953 in Edinburgh. He had been Prime Minister since 1997 and stepped down on 27 June 2007 – after his farewell tour. In his terms of office he has broken several records. After a modernisation of the Labour Party into what is now New Labour he was elected with what the official 10 Downing Street homepage calls "a landslide"[49] victory and became the youngest Prime Minister since Lord Liverpool in 1812. In 2001 he was re-elected "with another landslide majority" and in 2005 the Labour Party won the General Elections again, even though with a smaller margin, which meant another term of office for Mr Blair.

Blair is married to barrister Cherie Booth, QC. The couple have four children, the youngest of whom, Leo, "was the first child born to a serving Prime Minister in 150 years".[50]

Awareness

The three awareness tasks are highly subjective and aim not only at a review of what students experienced in their childhood, but also at the structures they live in. Individual answers are not only interesting in their own right, but must be seen in the context of contemporary family patterns. Who is the main breadwinner, who is the main carer, how is the distribution of labour organised in individual families? What forms of bonding can be observed?[51] Answers to these questions would assume differences in meaning depending on whether students live in nuclear or (possibly in rural areas more prevalent) extended families, whether they are part of one-parent (male or female[52]), patchwork (or reconstituted), lesbian or gay families or whether their families may even be – sadly – dysfunctional. In any case, these tasks additionally lend themselves to vocabulary work on social register.

Since the whole complex might be a sensitive area for some students, a viable alternative would be to carry out the discussion on a more objective level and refer to statistics. In Britain figures on different family set-ups and household structures can be obtained from the annually published General Household Survey, specifically from the subsection 'Living in Britain'.[53]

The Text

The text can be read in the context of a recent discussion in Germany about incentives to raise the currently very low birthrate, the location at which young children can get the best upbringing and the ensuing demand for more creches and kindergartens, as well as day schools. In addition to that supplements for young parents are increased if fathers take time off to look after their young children, too. Is Germany lagging behind Britain and other European countries with regard to family-friendly policies?

The feature story "The myth of Super Dad" was published in the *Sunday Times* of 13 April 2003. It focuses on the redefiniton of male gender roles, at a time when Tony Blair's New Labour Party[54] congratulated themselves on the discovery of new fatherhood in Britain. Against the background of the Employment Act 2002 in which rules and regulations for paid paternity leave are specified[55] the author looks – tongue in cheek – at various examples of fathers in Britain. Among the celebrity fathers presented in the article there are men like Bob Geldof, tv presenter Johnny Vaughan and Tony Blair. To cast some light on the latter the above-mentioned short biography might be useful.

In the article Tony Blair, who likes to present himself as a family man, talks about his children as any other father would, outlining some of the joys and some of the problems (ll. 21–30) that raising a family brings about. He also mentions some aspects of the division of labour between the Blair parents (ll. 41–43). The reader might well be surprised by this rather personal information on domesticity and the easy-going style in which Blair presents it.

Yet, if the reader doubts Blair's honesty, he will surely think that this is a media hype, as Tony Blair and his so-called spin doctors are well-known for their clever relationship with the media. The author claims that Blair had to "woo back waning female support for Labour" (ll. 33f.) and adds that it is impossible to "put the appearance of interviews with the prime minister down to happenstance" (ll. 79f.). So the role of the media in helping the creation of the new superdad must not be underestimated. In an interview with "*She*, the magazine for women who juggle their lives" (l. 32), Blair comes across as a juggler himself, juggling his duties as the political leader of the country with his roles as a father of four and a husband sharing his domestic duties with his wife.

---

[49] www.number-10.gov.uk
[50] s.o.
[51] A definition of bonding can be found in the *Students' Book* on p. 34.
[52] An interesting article on single mothers entitled 'Holding the baby: the truth about single mothers' was published in the *Sunday Times Magazine* on 28 July 1996, pp.18–25.
[53] www.statistics.gov.uk/ghs does not only offer statistics, but also definitions of social concepts.
[54] "New Labour" is an alternative branding for the Labour Party dating from a conference slogan first used by the Labour Party in 1994 which was later seen in a draft manifesto published by the party in 1996, called *New Labour, New Life For Britain* and presented by Labour as being the brand of the new reformed party.
[55] http://www.dti.gov.uk/employment/employment-legislation/employment-guidance/page17139.html

The photo of Blair with baby son Leo on his arm published in this article adds to the visualisation of his image as a modern father. The author draws a line to the New Labour Party manifesto which was published a year before Labour "swept into power" (l. 84) and propagated "modernity, egalitarianism and inclusivity" (ll. 87f.), but legally concentrated "on the rights of mothers (maternity leave, flexibility for working mums)" (ll. 93f.). In order to redress the balance fatherhood is the topic of the years 2002/2003 and the Labour government makes use of media coverage in their "trade department-funded magazine *Dad*, 'the magazine for new fathers'" (ll. 45 ff.). The subtitle of the magazine is ambiguous, as it could be addressed to men who have recently become fathers or at men who embody New Labour's trendy ideas of new fatherhood.

The text focuses on three types of men and their predominant characteristics:

(1) The New Man:
- Originates from the early nineties (117)
- Negative counterfoil was the exclusively consumer-orientated "yuppie" (118)
- Dressed in designer clothes; had riverside cocktail bars as his haunts (125f.)
- Drove fast, souped-up cars (125)
- Got up in the night to comfort his newborn baby (128)
- Pushed a pram through the park (129)
- Sensitive; discussed feelings with women (131)
- In advertising he is presented as "well-groomed, well-dressed thirtysomething" (135f.)
- New Man poster boy was Mark Perry, but the male model disgraced himself, when he prided himself on having been a lothario (156 ff.)

(2) The Smug Dad:
- Suffers from the Smug Dad Syndrome[56] (SDS) (169 ff.)
- Feeds/ holds/ changes nappies in public, but not at home (175f.)
- Demonstratively affectionate show-off (167f.)
- Plays ostentatiously in the park, especially in the presence of childless couples (178f.)
- Sports a buggy which is also pushed by Tom Cruise (180 ff.)
- Displays his morning tiredness competitively (184 ff.)
- Does not do the work, but talks about it in order to take the glory (202 ff.)

(3) The Super Dad:
- Spends serious quality time with his kids when he gets home (91)
- Can be the master of the universe as well (90)
- Is a mythical creature (217f.)
- Makes use of his right to two weeks' paid paternity leave (94f.)

However, against this background of British father types, the author refers to social and economic aspects which are more realistic than idealistic, when he characterises the everyday situation of British men: they have the longest working hours in Europe; less than 15% of young fathers have flexible working hours; only 3% of all male workers have a jobshare. He also quotes the founder of Britain's parenting website, www.mumsnet.com, who casts a critical look at the attitudes of British men, when she says, "I think a lot of men still think of raising children as women's work." (ll. 215f.)

Dylan Jones, the author of this article, seems to distrust New Labour's campaign for new fatherhood and, to a certain extent, Tony Blair's intentions, but his depiction of the new man and the smug dad are not uncritical either. Even though in his outline he seldom overtly criticises the characters and character types, his choice of words and ironic style render his criticism home to the reader. Irony can be detected in some exaggerations the author uses: e.g. "tiredness has become such a furiously competitive game of one-upmanship" (ll. 184 ff.), or "one of my arms was becoming longer than the other due to excessive midnight cradle rocking" (ll. 199f.), in sweeeping statements like "Smug Dads are everywhere." (l.184), in compound neologisms such as "touchy-feely" (l.116), "show-offy" (l. 168) or simply the fact that being a Smug Dad is turned into a syndrome which can be diagnosed (cf. ll. 169)

Criticism of Tony Blair – as it has already been mentioned – is mainly expressed in the author's suspicion that Blair's campaign is a media hype and that a cynic would suspect "that the new government legislation and interest in new fatherhood [was] simply a ploy to appeal, not to modern men, but to women voters" (ll. 219 ff.), which definitely reveals the author to be a cynic. But the author, who includes himself among the readership of the article, seems to want to detect a streak of vanity in Blair who at the age of 50 "obviously feels the need to impress upon us the fact that he is family man at heart" (ll. 10 ff.). Later in the text the author makes it quite clear that he has put the prime minister into the box of Smug Dad (ll. 162f.). Could this be some male rivalry, as the author himself admits that at some point in his life he was a smug dad and "after all, a typical man, not a new man at all, not even a new lad. And certainly not a superdad." (ll. 204f.) Even though his confession sounds rather fetching, the author seems to think that it reflects the normal attitude of men, shrugging shoulders because they cannot help themselves. So why should Tony Blair be different?

In these days of mass media presence with their power and influence on the increase the public image of a politician or celebrity is of supreme importance. An

---

[56] In addition to ist medical meaning the DCE defines syndrome as "a set of qualities, events, or types of behaviour that is typical of a particular kind of problem".

Internet dictionary defines 'image' as a fictitious concept of an object which is shared collectively. In this case the "object" is the prime minister and the term refers to the collective public opinion such a person is confronted with and how this public opinion can be influenced, if not manipulated by, e.g., advisers to this public figure. In Tony Blair's case we frequently talk about his spin doctors who shape his public image. The article creates the image of a father who makes use of his paternal role to bring home the impression that he is a man just like his male voters and a model of fatherhood for his female voters. Semiotically the signs he has encoded must be interpreted like that. If the voter looks at him critically he will realize that what Tony Blair presents has been constructed. If the reader were to deconstruct his public image he would probably notice that – as Dylan Jones maintains – "while it would be unfair to say that Blair exploited his family unit it won't have escaped anyone's notice that his family has helped enormously with his public image (ll. 163 ff.).

Project

11 Quality time is spent with one's children, when one is at leisure to give them full attention. In the past presumably mothers were the contacts most closely connected with children and most likely to spend lots of time with them. When working mums became ubiquitous, quality time first referred to them, possibly to alleviate their guilt complexes. With concepts of new fatherhood quality time for fathers has become a wider issue. Students could come up with plenty of ideas in group work as to structure the quality time spent with children to the latters' benefit. Other ideas can be found in the Internet if you consult www.fatherhood. The Internet page mentions 10 ways to spend quality time with kids:

1. Tell them a story.
2. Plan a picnic.
3. Take a vacation.
4. Turn off the TV.
5. Spend the evening together.
6. Grow a garden.
7. Eat together.
8. Help with homework.
9. Enjoy the cold weather.
10. Hit the road.[57]

Internet Projects

Britain's parenting website (by parents for parents) www.mumsnet.com deals with all topics related to becoming/being parents, has got offers for all kinds of products related to babies/toddlers and offers the opportunity to chat about such topics as hypnobirthing, alpha mums and helping to find Madeleine[58].

Men will find an update on fashion, grooming and style in the Internet pages www.men.style.com and will get advice on what to wear on a summer's evening, but are also invited to enrol for a subscription to GQ (the editor of which – ironically – is Dylan Jones).

The Cartoon

The cartoon on p. 40 takes an ironic look at paternity leave. The couple are obviously planning to start a family and the father-to-be is working out when to go on paternity leave with the help of a sports calendar. The year is 2006, which gives it additional meaning as it was the year of the soccer world championship, and from personal experience I know that there was a lot of enthusiasm all over Britain (albeit not only amongst men).

Where Do We Go from Here?

11 | Fun Quiz: Are you hetero, metro or completely off the dial?

text type: (newspaper) quiz/questionnaire
length: 1024 words
degree of difficulty: ***, 20 annotations; 28 explanations
theme: recent trends in male gender roles
teaching points: (gender) patterns in questionnaires; role expectations; British popular culture

related visual material: photo of well-groomed man; photo of surfer; two cartoons about recent trends in gender roles

Awareness

Psychological tests are a feature of a great number of weekly or monthly magazines. Even if students claim that they are never tempted to do them, they may well be able to speculate on the motivations of those who feel the 'compulsion' to do them. A lot of people have more time for such activities at the dentist's or the hairdresser's than anywhere else. In the former situation they are probably nervous and need an easy pastime to distract their minds. Admittedly, it is also tempting to find out about one's 'true' self by answering a few simple questions in a short time. So this type of psychological

---

[57] Check www.fatherhood.about.com/od/activities/tp/quality_time.htm

[58] Madeleine is a 4-year-old girl who was kidnapped from a holiday resort in Portugal.

test opens an instant road to painless, inexpensive self-recognition. You neither need courage nor must you make a great effort. It is fascinating to compare the results of your scoring with your self-image. If the description in the test is better than your self-image, you feel flattered; if it is worse, you can discard the entire test as irrelevant without any negative effects on your ego.

The Text

Semiotically speaking the quiz is a text, since it is a meaningful sign configuration. What is unusal and adds to the funny aspect is the fact that the questions exclusively refer to different male gender roles and not to the quite common distinction between male/female behaviour and role expectations. The headline of the quiz is humorous not only because of the short forms of the words hetero and metro, which presupposes that these words are known to the reader/testee, but also because it employs a climactic order with the phrase "completely off the dial" in top position leaving the reader's/testee's expectations frustrated as he is trying to make sense of the expression. The definitions of terms have to be taken in turn.

The DCE defines heterosexual as "sexually attracted to people of the opposite sex". Wikipedia defines metro~ in the following way: **Metrosexual** is a word describing men who have a strong concern for their aesthetic appearance, and spend a substantial amount of time and money on their *images* (italics mine) and lifestyles. Though the term has undergone a transformation from its original meaning (a heterosexual man who appeared or acted as if he were homosexual or bisexual), current trends have seen the metrosexual label placed upon male embracing of practices usually perceived to be feminine, rather than those specifically associated with stereotypically effeminate homosexuals. Debate surrounds the term's use as a theoretical signifier of gender deconstruction and its associations with consumerism. Current gender scholars view **metrosexuality** as representative of the embracing of relational understanding in addition to its lifestyle and aesthetic implications.

"The typical metrosexual is a young man with money to spend, living in or within easy reach of a metropolis – because that's where all the best shops, clubs, gyms and hairdressers are. He might be officially gay, straight or bisexual, but this is utterly immaterial because he has clearly taken himself as his own love object and pleasure as his sexual preference. Particular professions, such as modeling, waiting tables, media, pop music and, nowadays, sport, seem to attract them but, truth be told, like male vanity products and herpes, they're pretty much everywhere." (Mark Simpson, "Meet the metrosexual," Salon.com, July 22, 2002)

The promotion of metrosexuality was left to the men's style press, magazines such as The Face, *GQ* (italics mine), Esquire, Arena and FHM, the new media which took off in the Eighties and is still growing (GQ gains 10,000 new readers every month). They filled their magazines with images of narcissistic young men sporting fashionable clothes and accessories, and they persuaded other young men to study them with a mixture of envy and desire.

The figurehead of metrosexuality in Britain has been David Beckham. When he was captain of the English soccer team it was rather ironic that a metrosexual should be in a leading position in a sport which is overwhelmingly laddish and attracts British machos who adhere to values as propagated in the sitcom *Men Behaving Badly* (see text 12 in the *Students' Book*). "Beckham has helped break "masculine codes", says Warwick University sociology professor Dr Andrew Parker, "defying various manly expectations such as what clothes a man is allowed to wear".[59]

The third term tops it all: 'to be completely off the dial' means 'to be incalculable' (see annotations) which is probably intended to leave options open for further development, cuts across all cliché-ridden attempts at gender stereotyping and has the reader/testee flirt with the idea that gender is entirely a matter of personal choice.

The concepts of masculinity employed in the test obviously go from one end of the spectrum to the other. One of the polar opposites describes machismo behaviour whereas the other features an imitation of female behaviour. The concept of machismo reveals a man whose behaviour is traditionally masculine. Masculinity refers to socially acquired traits of behaviour, e.g. men do not cry, but remain calm and in control. They do outdoor sports – football and hunting among other activities – go to the pub and do not talk about emotions.

Janet Saltzman Chafetz (1974) describes seven areas of masculinity in general culture:

1. Physical – virile, athletic, strong, brave. Unconcerned about appearance and aging;
2. Functional – breadwinner, provider for family as much as mate;
3. Sexual – sexually aggressive, experienced. Single status acceptable;
4. Emotional – unemotional, stoic, don't cry;
5. Intellectual – logical, intellectual, rational, objective, practical;
6. Interpersonal – leader, dominating; disciplinarian; independent, free, individualistic; demanding;

---

[59] Peter Gotting, *Rise of the Metrosexual*, March 11, 2003 (www.theage.com.au)

7. Other Personal Characteristics – success-oriented, ambitious, aggressive, proud, egotistical; moral, trustworthy; decisive, competitive, uninhibited, adventurous.[60]

A number of the above-mentioned qualities can be found in the first category of masculinity, i.e. the man who rated *mostly As*:
- He is keen on football and rugby.
- He goes to pubs and strip joints.
- He watches pornography.
- He does not attach any importance to his outward appearance and is not interested in fashion.
- He is neither diet- nor health-conscious.
- He tries to 'resolve' some conflicts with violence.
- His taste in music is predominantly 'Heavy Metal'.
- He cannot stand homosexuals.

The man who has scored *mostly Bs*:
- He goes to a barber, rather than a hairdresses.
- Though he hugs a male friend, his hug is 'manly'.
- Though he does not pay much attention to his outward appearance, he occasionally uses an aftershave.
- He is more interested in sports than in drinking.
- He loves to discuss sports and results of matches.
- He compromises, even in critical situations.
- He is tolerant towards homosexuals.
- Interested in, though not necessarily part of the lad culture.

The man who rated *mostly Cs*:
- He knows a lot about cosmetics and fashions.
- He goes to a hairdresser rather than a barber.
- He cares for his skin and outward appearance in general.
- He frequents bars rather than pubs, and prefers cocktails to beers.
- He is well informed about designer labels, trendy colours and accessories.
- He admires gays for their style.
- He discusses art.
- His taste in music includes Dido.

The man who rated *mostly Ds*:
- He has his hair done in a salon.
- He has got a big array of different cosmetics.
- He has got exquisite tastes.
- He likes rugby, but because of the rugby players' legs.
- He admires the outfit of cross-dressing men.
- He uses some affected phraes.
- His taste in music includes Gloria Gaynor (two songs of whom have become hymns among the gay community).
- He is a gossip.

The style in which the questionnaire is presented is mostly colloquial (expressions like wimp (l. 33), hissy fit (l. 69), fry-up (l. 162) etc.), verging on the impolite (e.g. cissy (l. 3), bloody (l. 94)). There are also some humorous expressions like "… you'll be needing evening primrose oil soon" (l. 182), "Eat your heart out, …" (l. 178), trap two (ll. 162f.). The sentence structure is often elliptical, which originates from the pattern of a statement or a question at the beginning of each entry followed by a list of four choices. These lists add to the humour of the quiz, because they contain a lot of exaggeration, with one of markers being way out (see No. 18), or they offer choices which at first sight seem to have nothing to do with each other (see No. 21) so that they have to be contextualised. All in all this quiz is not only a fantastic help for presenting male gender roles in a tongue-in-cheek manner, but also a good form of bringing idiomatic vocabulary home to the student at the same time as providing a vast amount of cultural background information.

Project 6

Each of the four diary entries will offer interesting approaches to taxing student creativity.

"Mostly A" could spend a day at a rugby or football match and could experience a lot of (macho-)male bonding.

"Mostly B" could take his mother to a Shirley Bassey concert or write about his experiences as best man at a Scottish wedding.

"Mostly C" could go on a shopping spree after which he could drift into a trendy bar.

"Mostly D" could be sent to a spa and experience all the paraphernalia of wellness and grooming.

Cartoons

The cartoon on p. 45 displays a reversal of traditional gender stereotypes. While the woman in front of the bathroom mirror seems rather cool in her verbal behaviour, the man in the bathtub 'is crying'. The irony behind his sensitive softness is that he is crying because he has got soap in his eyes, which changes his tears into a childish reaction. So the cartoon obviously makes fun of the man's pretended sensitivity.

The cartoon on p. 46 puts emphasis on the similarities of gender with metrosexual implications. The term 'androgeny' in the first bubble refers to a happy harmony between male and female elements. This harmonious atmosphere is "topped" by the woman's attempt at borrowing a lipstick from one of the metrosexual males.

---

[60] quoted in Wikipedia under the heading of masculinity

12 "The new ladette or: Call my bluff?"*

text type: newspaper article (interpretive news story)
length: 1036 words
degree of difficulty: **, 36 annotations;
11 explanations;
theme: a personally teinted description of changed behavioral patterns among contemporary British young women
teaching points: reasons for and causes of behavioral patterns; role expectations; pc English; irony; style in newspaper articles

related visual material: cartoon showing bad behaviour in a henhouse

additional material: info box on lad/ladette culture, p. 49

Background

In the last decade of the 20th century trends in popular culture – among other areas reflected in literature – became noticeable which were not entirely in line with even trendy gender role expectations. In popular literature the trends of chic and lad literature were initiated with the publication of novels like Helen Fielding's *Bridget Jones's Diary*[61] or Nick Hornby's *Fever Pitch*[62] as well as new men's magazine called *Loaded*[63]. These were accompanied by incredibly popular sitcoms, e.g. *Men behaving badly* or *Sex in the City*[64] which became trendsetters and alerted not only their fans to "the dynamic state of gender relations".[65] Their male/female stars were even considered to be role models for what was deemed appropriate behaviour. In this context a number of synonyms are used which refer basically to the same phenomena reflected in chic/lad lit, behaviour and language: lad/ladette or chavo/chavette.[66] In this context the BBC tv comedy series *Little Britain* must be mentioned as one of its main characters, Vicky Pollard (played by Matt Lucas), has been modelled into the epitome of a Chavette. Their behavioral as well as linguistic patterns can be likened to a phenomenon which in urban geography has been called the 'proletarianisation' of inner-city areas, in other words an adherence to standards which are not middle-class and could be classified as down-market despite the fact that middle/upper-class accessories are sported. The language, style and patterns of behaviour of those who adher to this popular culture send out different signals, however. For examples see any of the below-mentioned publications.

Awareness

1 Students may refer to personal experiences and the result of their "soul-searching" could be that young women tend to be more assertive than young men of the same age, as the former develop faster, while young men are probably more assertive later in their adolescence. What is more, the influence of alcohol consumption must be considered in both genders.

2 Signs declaring alcohol consumption to be an offence have become a fixture of British (seaside) towns. They are intended to reduce alcohol abuse and prevent its consequences, such as smashed-up bottles and glasses, vandalism or unruly behaviour causing disturbance to local residents and holiday-makers. Recent studies have documented that binge-drinking has become an alarming feature of popular youth culture, not only in Britain.

3 The list of adjectives to be compiled by students could contain the following:
Adventurous, aggressive, arrogant, assertive, bashful, boisterous, considerate, demure, disciplined, dominant, domestic, energetic, fickle, fragile, introvert, sensible, sensitive, strong, submissive, talkative, warm-hearted, weak, undecided etc.

It will be interesting to compare lists compiled by boys with those compiled by girls and to discuss the differences.

The text

The author maintains that crime rates among women are on the increase at an ever faster pace so that even though men still commit more crimes the gap is getting narrower (ll. 7 ff.). As alcohol abuse is one of the reasons for criminal behaviour, the fact that the gender gap in drinking is also dwindling adds to the increase in crime rates among women (ll. 9 ff.). The types of drinks consumed reveal that women do not restrict themselves to "classic" women's drinks like Babycham – a well-known "female" drink in post-war Britain, officially launched in 1953 – but consume "male" tipples such as lager or ale (ll. 15 ff.). In that respect the gender gap has been closed – according to findings by the Brewers' and Licensed Retailers' Association (ll. 13 ff.).

Another moment of revelation presented itself in the 1994 Miss UK/Mr UK beauty contest which highlighted almost reversed behavioral patterns among male and female spectators. While women reacted to male models "with screams of appreciation and suggestive remarks" (ll. 33f.), female contestants were met with "polite applause from the demure, bashful males" (l. 36). This

---

[61] London, 1996. Later a film version attracted a wide audience.
[62] London, 1992
[63] first published 1994
[64] All of the previous quoted in: Katharine Cockin, "Chicks and Lads in Contemporary British Fiction", anglistik & englischunterricht, 2007, Bd. 69, pp. 107-123.
[65] a.a.O., p. 107
[66] Various publications present an interesting ironic overview:
Lee Bok, The Chav Guide to Life (Cheam, 2006)
Lee Bok, The Little Book of Chavs (Cheam, 1st edition 2004)
Lee Bok, The Little Book of Chav Jokes (Cheam, 2006)
Lee Bok, The Little Book of Chav Speak (Cheam, 1st edition 2004)

change in manners, i.e. women being more forward and demonstrative than men, has also been noticed by some male and female popstars in their fans (ll. 38–47).

In previous generations young women were expected to be bashful, coy and demure, especially in their relations with the opposite gender, to which (according to the author) the developments of feminism and pc linguistic behaviour added serious and sobering touches. Young women nowadays are allowed to express their femaleness (l. 82), at the same time claiming for themselves that they can be as free and extrovert as men. In our fun-oriented society they demand their share of fun and sneer at pc terminology. According to Angela Holden, author of *Sky magazine*, "young women are tired of being the standard-bearers for political correctness [...]" (ll. 72f.).

A new dress code has added to these revolutionary forms of self-determination. The text reveals the "Wonderbra phenomenon [to be] a true sign of the times" (ll. 86ff.). While in the past girls were brought up not to show their bra straps, they nowadays not only show their bra straps under skimpy tank tops, but bare their midriffs and also reveal pierced navels. However, the author maintains that young women's behaviour rejects the idea of victimisation and can be evaluated as a form of self-expression. What was reserved for men in the past is now expressed "in a manner that is undeniably feminine" (ll. 90 ff.).

The male author of the text welcomes the changes in the young women of today for several reasons: he appreciates their new self-confidence and even the negative aspects of their behaviour as they cast a new light on men who – in public opinion – seem to have had the monopoly on badness. He claims that women's new "commitment to bad behaviour destroys for once and for all the notion that there is something uniquely bestial about the male psyche" (ll. 105 ff.). But it also causes the author to empathise with the girls, as he knows from experience that there is a streak of insecurity involved in this demonstratively self-confident behaviour. Both, men and women, find themselves under a lot of peer pressure, the underpinning similarity being that he is "all mouth and no trousers" (l. 118), whilst she is "all mouth and no miniskirt" (l. 119). This phenomenon has to be borne in mind in the ultimate characterisation of the ladette: she is extrovert, drinks a lot, seems invinceably self-confident, reveals a repertoire of semi-provocative behaviour, especially when she is in her peer group, but underneath it all she is definitely somewhat insecure.

The article is an interpretive news story which draws the reader's attention to a current phenomenon. The author does not only provide the reader with bare facts, but places them into a wider social context, adds background information as well as his personal opinion. The current phenomenon is that of the ladette culture, which can be observed in British streets all the time; the wider social context is that of changing codes of behaviour, the background information is provided in the form of statistics collected by the AA (l. 3), the Brewers' and Licensed Retailers' Association and in a marketing study (ll. 21 ff.), as well as research carried out by *Sky magazine* (ll. 48 ff.) and a survey on Wild Women (ll. 110 ff.). The author's opinion is overtly expressed and placed – undisputed and without any restrictions – at the end of the article so that the reader is clearly expected to adopt it.

The style in which the article is written is predominantly colloquial, spiced up with a slang expression:

Colloquial style:	**Slang expression:**
well (ll. 1, 10)	male journo-pigs (l. 61)
direct address of the reader (l. 1)	
babes, chicks, blokes (are quotations from the ladettes' register)	
beefy hunk (l. 29)	
naff (l. 50)	
faux-blokes (l. 26)	
phrases like: all mouth and no trousers (l. 118)	
incomplete sentence (ll. 19f.)	
rhetorical questions (ll. 9f., 26)	

This lively style makes the article entertaining and helps to attract the reader's attention to this new social phenomenon.

If one did not know the author's name, it would not be clear from the beginning whether the text has been written by a man or a woman. However, in ll. 27–37 there is a slight bias in favour of male behaviour despite the fact that it is not in line with the reader's expectations. The author's gender becomes more obvious in his explanation of what he terms the "Wonderbra phenomenon", i.e. that it shows "triumphs of mammary engineering" (ll. 89f.). The concept of engineering seems to be male rather than female.

When the author sets himself off from other men the reader can see that he is a new, liberal male, but the most obvious signs can be found when he puts forth the reasons for his inherent support to and admiration of the ladettes (ll. 104f.) and his understanding of what it means to be under (peer-)pressure (ll. 117–120).

The Cartoon

The cartoon on p. 48 is a wonderful satire on gross male chat-up lines, which becomes blatantly ironic in the setting of a henhouse and against the background of the hens' behaviour. In the henhouse, which is full of beer cans and wine bottles, the hens/women copy rather crude cockish/male forms of verbal behaviour and body language. Additional aspects of irony can be detected in the caption "hen behaving badly" which is a pun on the title of the sitcom *Men behaving badly*, but also refers to the custom of notorious hen nights on which women only celebrate a boozy and often unruly farewell to a female friend who is getting married. The male equivalent is a stag party celebrated in the same style. For both genders it is their so-called last night of freedom, and sociologically speaking the event is a rite of passage to married life.

While in the past these events took place in a local pub, the venue nowadays tends to be abroad in locations like the Czech Republic, Poland or Latvia, where alcohol is cheap and travel expenses are low. An estimated 30,000 young Britons visited Prague in 2006.[67] "Riga has become particularly popular with British stag parties looking for cheap alcohol, beautiful women and casual sex."[68] Young Latvians who have staged a protest campaign have invented the neologism "sex terrorists" who have made Riga "the Bangkok of the Baltic".[69] The interesting point made in the Sunday Times article is that according to a spokesman of a local planning association it is not only money that seduces Latvian women, but also "the chat-up lines of foreign men. 'It's a cultural difference. Latvian men rarely pay women compliments or give them much attention.'"[70]

Bearing in mind the importance of chat-up lines students could be asked to translate "hen speak" into human language. According to the DCE the clucking of chickens describes a low short noise, but clucking rhymes with f***ing which would be very much in line with a crude chat-up line. The noun pecker is also ambiguous, as in old-fashioned British English it means mouth/chin, whereas in informal American English it means penis.

Another ambiguous term from "hen speak" is "to ruffle s.o.'s feathers". In human language it could translate into to ruffle s.o.'s hair which is the equivalent to smoothing s.o.'s hair affectionately, but in human language the term to ruffle s.o.'s feathers means to offend s.o., which ties in with these rather offensive chat-up lines.

A list of examples of chat-up lines can be found in *The Little Book of Chav Speak* by Lee Bok, which ostensibly provides "the latest hip lingo that's hitting the streets".[71]

All in all this cartoon provides a motivating link with Project 12 in which students will be asked to devise their own chat-up lines for the opposite gender.

---

[67] Klaus Brill, "Rüpel statt Gentlemen: Plagegeister von der Insel", *Süddeutsche Zeitung*, 17. Juli 2007
[68] Nicola Smith, Gary Peach, "Sex-tourism revolt in the 'Bangkok of the Baltic'", *The Sunday Times*, July 1, 2007, p.27
[69] ibid.
[70] ibid.
[71] a.a.O., back cover

Additional websites

The phenomenon of lads and ladettes has had widespread media coverage. Try these additional websites:

uk.tickle.com/test/**ladette**.html – This test answers to the stringent question "Are you a ladette or a lady?"

domino.lancs.ac.uk/info/lunews.nsf/I gives information about the rise of the ladette culture at British schools.

news.bbc.co.uk/1/hi/uk/1434906.stm provides information about the recognotion of the term and the concept of ladettes bin dictionaries.

A plethora of websites offer venues and event management for hen- or stag nights in Britain and abroad.

13 | "A bad victory for women"

text type: newspaper article (feature story)
length: 1114 words
degree of difficulty: **; 32 annotations and 5 explanations
theme: sexual harassment
teaching points: work ethics; irony; elements of subjective argumentation; reactions to (sexual) harassment

related visual material: two cartoons about equal pay, cartoon of a board meeting "And we'd have someone to grope!!"; poster of car advertisement with graffiti

background reading 1 and 2 about sexual harassment, p. 53, and equality at work, p. 54; Info Box about Sexism, p. 55

Background

The Equal Opportunities Commission (EOC) was established by Parliament in 1975, the year in which the Sex Discrimination Act was enforced. The purpose of the EOC is to ensure that men and women have the same chances in education and employment, and that they are treated fairly and equally by their teachers, employers, etc. The EOC is frequently involved in legal cases to claim and maintain the basic principle of equal rights for men and women. The Commission is funded by grants from the Employment Department, yet they do not see themselves as a government body. They feel independent enough to criticize government policy, where necessary. Moreover, they issue leaflets, offer a forum for employers with good equal opportunities management practices, alert policy-makers and opinion-formers, and spread information about latest developments by means of conferences, seminars and training programmes. Research and statistical work is undertaken by the Commission, too. What is important for individual employees is that the Commission operates at the grass roots and gives support to those who might not feel powerful enough to fend for themselves.

For a long time sexual harassment was a grey area, because nobody – neither the judiciary, nor those who suffered from it – was prepared to take the topic up or had the strength to see it through. Even after legislation on the basis of the Sex Discrimination Act of 1975, it is still a critical decision for employees to take a complaint to court and have their rights secured at the possible expense of losing their job. Despite legislation it is still a sensitive area, and some employees may be motivated to remain silent rather than speak up for themselves.

Sexual harassment may cover a wide area and can be defined in more ways than one, from minor forms to major offences and owing to a varying tolerance threshold what is still tolerable to one victim may be totally unacceptable to another. A number of cases – some with sensational press coverage – have been made known to the public in the U.S. and GB so that by and large there has been a sensitization for the problem.

Awareness

The topic of sexual harassment is dealt with satirically in the two illustrations on pp. 54 ff. of the *Students' Book*.

The picture on p. 54 could easily be turned into a fantasy tale, or even a modern fable. In the car dealer's showroom the new, wonderfully good-looking Fiat is repeatedly told that it looks like a lady and has all the positive attributes the potential customer associates with a lady. So it is quite happy to leave the showroom and be part of an advertisement on the billboard, because it thinks that this is its destiny. But at night in the dark, it misses all the other little 'Fiat ladies' from the showroom. To counteract its feeling of loneliness it steps out of the billboard and turns into a beautiful blonde lady, who attracts the attention of all the male passers-by. She walks down the road, as if on a catwalk, and admires her reflexion in one of the big department store windows. A passer-by, who observes this act of self-admiration, surreptitiously reaches out and pinches the lady's bottom. Taken aback with shock and fury, she steps out into the street to get away from her harasser. In the course of this event her identity changes back to that of a little Fiat. She pursues her harasser and ruthlessly runs him down.

When the Fiat wakes up in the morning it is part of the billboard again, but, unfortunately, its abode has been soiled by graffiti.

Moral: Take it with a pinch of salt!

The cartoon on p. 56 might be 'translated' as follows: During the board meeting of the managing directors of an insurance company, the human resources manager tells his colleagues about the applicants shortlisted for the vacant position of accountant. Five people have the qualifications requested, one of whom is a woman. In the discussion that follows the pros and cons of the individual applicants are juxtaposed. Eventually, the board of directors valiantly decides to employ the woman. The human resources manager delightedly declares this to be a good idea, since the Prime Minister has after all voiced a strong opinion in favour of the employment and promotion of qualified women. Even the managing director, known to be a chauvinist, is delighted. When the board members express their amazement at this change of attitude, the managing director smirks and says they might as well have some well-deserved fun with someone to grope.

The following morning, as the managing director is walking down the executives' corridor, he can feel a hand groping **his** bottom. He screams 'blue murder', but then he hears a very quiet female voice saying, "Don't do unto others what you don't want to have done unto yourself".

In order to decide where to draw the line between flattery and offence students might think of the following situations:
- workmen whistling at a building-site,
- men looking women up and down, clicking their tongues and saying "Look at that"!,
- male colleagues putting their arms around female colleagues when they are in a group,
- a man putting his hand on a woman's knee,
- bottom-pinching,
- telling 'tit and bum' jokes or 'silly blonde' jokes in the company of women,
- stalking (which is the crime of following someone over a period of time in order to force them to have sex or kill them; this crime has had a lot of media coverage in the U.S.),
- sexual molesting, etc.

The Text

India Knight is known – among other accomplishments – for her weekly column in the *Sunday Times*, in which she comments on a multitude of subjects, most of which cover highly topical issues, hot off the press. She always voices decided opinions, which – more often than not – differ from mainstream ideas. So her articles are full of surprises to those readers who think they have pigeonholed her.

In the article "A bad victory for women" she tells the story of Wall Street banker Laura Zubulake who sued her employer for sex discrimination and won the equivalent of £15.6m in compensation. Rather than congratulating Ms Zubulake on her deal and considering it a victory over a male bastion that does not deserve any better, the author reproaches her with behaving like a sensitive little flower (see l. 43) and not "like a grown-up" (l. 84), even doing harm to the reputation of women in general, which can be concluded from the title of the article and the author's advice that "she should pipe down about the great service she has done sisterhood" (ll. 108f.). The author claims that if you work in a male bastion like Wall Street (NYC) or the City of London (which, the author claims, are much the same except that less compensation money is paid in London), the law courts and even Fleet Street (see ll. 41f.), the working atmosphere will be tough and the woman who claims equal rights cannot afford to be wanting extra-sensitive treatment at the same time. If she has risen to the challenge, she will have to take the rough with the smooth. The work ethic suggested by India Knight is that any woman working in such capacity should behave like a grown-up, which she paraphrases several times: to her it means accepting and "confronting the realities of equality" (l. 88) "warts and all" (l. 85), but also "dealing with [the problem] like a man" (l. 87). She detects a tendency of weakness in women "to be […] all mouth and no trousers" (l. 90), and thus not to be fit for the clout in male bastions. The author even detects something like double standards in women who claim that they "want to be treated equally" (l. 77) and when "they are teased and bullied as equals, they run screaming to the courts" (ll. 78f.).

The men who work in such environments are, as the author puts it, "often mad, sad and greedy" (l. 94), in other words fiercely competitive, exceedingly ambitious, likely to tell each other off-colour jokes and tend to go to the pub or a strip-joint (with or without clients) after work. So all in all these are not "wildly women-friendly environments" (l. 38). But, women do know what to expect, if they decide to work with these men.

In her feature story the author draws a very negative character sketch of Laura Zubulake, presenting her as an employee who complains a lot, not always about issues which are justified (ll. 61–70), does not really know what she wants, when first she is "appalled" that she has been asked "to join colleagues and clients at a strip-joint" (ll. 58f.) and later she is dismayed that she is not (see ll. 65f.). The author describes the banker as "triumphant" (l. 8) and "jubilant" (l. 107) about her success, but it does not find Knight's approval even though she concedes that Zubulake "has had the last laugh, […] financially" (ll. 105f.), but she evaluates it as detrimental to the cause of women, and thus she does not see it as any victory at all.

The language the author uses reveals her harsh criticism of Ms Zubulake and her attitudes. She asks some ironic rhetorical questions about her (see ll. 27 ff., ll. 49f.) and about equivalent male behaviour (ll. 30–35). She makes Ms Zubulake's case look unjust, when she calls her legal complaint "mimsy" (l. 52) and uses parenthesis to comment on her behavior (ll. 59f., l. 64, l. 68).

The author also employs a lot of irony to make her opinion of Ms Zubulake clear to the reader. As her style of writing is predominantly colloquial, the irony suits it very well and the article could even be part of a conversation. When she marvels at the amount of money Zubulake earns and is granted as compensation, she comments on it with "Oh, please." (l. 29) and adds in order to deserve it "You'd really have to be called an awful lot of names." (l. 19) She also mentions survival techniques in a man's world in ironic style, when she says that a woman has "to develop the hide of an especially robust rhinoceros" (ll. 46f.). The overall tone is one of irony and pretended pity for a woman who is such a high earner that she should know how to fend for herself.

The Cartoons

The cartoons on pp. 51 and 52 both deal with the topic of equal pay. In the first cartoon a male boss tells his female employee that the company pay her less because they are men. The message is that many a bigoted explanation has been found in the long history of unequal pay to justify the policy.

In the second cartoon the secretary has obviously interpreted the policy of equal pay in her favor and expects the same salary as her boss, which he refuses to comply with.

14 | Adriaane Pielou "Prattle of the sexes"

text type: newspaper article (feature)
length: 870 words
degree of difficulty: *; 32 annotations and 1 explanation
theme: gender-based language difference
teaching points: socio-linguistic aspects in the gender discussion; psychology of men and women

related visual material: book cover

Background

"Speech is an act of identity: when we speak, one of the things we do is identify ourselves as male or female."[72] This insight is by no means new. Otto Jespersen published some interesting research results as early as 1925. "Es soll volksstämme geben, in welchen die männer und die weiber völlig verschiedene sprachen oder jedenfalls abweichende dialekte reden."[73] Apparently, it was recorded in the 17th century that among a tribe on one of the islands of the Antilles in the Caribbean Sea men and women spoke different language varieties. "[Die] männer haben eine große zahl nur ihnen eigentümlicher ausdrücke, welche die frauen wohl verstehen, niemals aber selbst in den mund nehmen. Auf der anderen seite verfügen die frauen über wörter und redensarten, die die männer niemals anwenden, denn sonst verfielen sie dem fluch der lächerlichkeit."[74]

---

[72] J. Coates, *Women, Men and Language* (London: Longman, 1986), quoted in: *Language and Social Life*, ed. by Martin Montgomery and Helen Reid-Thomas (London: The British Council, 1994), p. 23.
[73] Otto Jespersen, "Die frau.", in: *Die Sprache* (Heidelberg, 1925), p. 48.
[74] See Jespersen, ibid.

Communication was difficult in that situation, but according to Jesperson not impossible. An interesting aspect mentioned in the original text is that if a man chooses the wrong code he lays himself open to ridicule. One might conclude that such a man would have been considered to be effeminate. In other words, there must be interdependencies between gender role expectations and the linguistic codes that are used by members of the opposite sex.

One of the most frequently cited cases where there are striking differences between women's and men's usages is the Japanese language. Here the bulk of sex-differentiated frequencies in the use of particular forms can be explained in terms of women speaking more politely than men. Differences in politeness-level play a role in expressing gender-identity. A linguist has noted, however, that high frequencies of certain particles connected to politeness and formality (so-called 'women's language') are much more likely to occur in certain contexts, e.g. a young woman talking to a male classmate at a social event will speak far more "politely" than when talking to that same young man in a classroom setting. Older women, on the other hand, use these forms far less often than they did in the courtship and early marriage stages of their lives.[75] From this, as from many other examples in the gender discussion may be concluded that simplified labels obscure rather then enlighten.

Awareness

For this and the other communicative exercises in the context of text 14, it might be a good idea to have mixed male-female groups.

The title of this text is obviously a pun on the concept of the battle of the sexes. The word "prattle" connotes incessant childish, meaningless, or unimportant talk. It is used for the chatter of both men and women.

Differences between male and female language varieties can be found in all areas of the grammar of English, and also students' native languages. Areas to be mentioned in detail are lexical items, syntax, intonation and pitch, but also extra-linguistic traits such as different body language. To identify the differences is not as easy at it seems and one must be careful to avoid clichés. Examples quoted again and again are: the use of tag questions (women are said to use them and phrases like 'you know' much more frequently than men); the use of expletives (men are said to use stronger expletives than women, e.g. 'shit' rather than 'oh dear'); polite forms of request (women's speech is said to sound more polite than men's, e.g. 'Please close the door.' – rather than – 'Close the door!'); the use of intensifiers (females are said to use more intensifiers, e.g. 'so,' 'such,' 'quite,' 'vastly'); patterns of hesitation (women are said to use 'well' more frequently than men and to be interrupted more in conversation, while men are the more successful interrupters). In mixed-sex groups men talk more and are more successful at initiating topics. "Empirical studies of nonverbal communication and of address forms show similar phenomena: not surprisingly, men tend to communicate with women as the socially powerful communicate with those whom they dominate."[76]

In addition, there are conceptual patterns which reflect male and female roles in language: men bellow; women purr; men yell; women scream; men get angry; women have tantrums; married women engage in 'homemaking;' single women 'keep house;' men have careers; women have jobs (the term 'career woman' still has negative connotations).

The Text

The American linguist Deborah Tannen was interviewed by Adrianne Pielou to make the results of the former's research known to a large British (non-academic) readership. Tannen is considered to be an authority on male-female differences of talk, and her publication *You Just Don't Understand: Men and Women in Conversation* has become an international bestseller because it is easy to understand due to the absence of otherwise wide-spread linguistic jargon.

Deborah Tannen makes use of an episode, in which a married couple in a car lose their way, as a simple, but crucial example to reveal the differences in male-female speaking, thinking and feeling. Tannen's main tenets are that women tend to speak and hear a language of connection and intimacy, while men men speak and hear a language of status and independence. In the car episode these contradictory approaches inevitably lead to a conflict. Though this contretemps seems totally unnecessary to an outsider, its psychological build-up proves that it is deeply ingrained in the male-female psyche. Tannen does not take sides; nor does she tell men and women how to behave differently in future. She merely observes and reports. Yet her seemingly clear-

---

[75] Sally McConnell-Ginet, "Linguistics and the Feminist Challenge," in: *Women and Language in Literature and Society*, ed. by Sally McConnell-Ginet/Ruth Borker/Nelly Furman (New York, 1980), p. 19.

[76] See Nancy Henley, Body Politics (Englewood Cliffs, N.J.: Prentice-Hall, 1977), quoted in Sally McConnell-Ginet, "Linguistics and the Feminist Challenge," in: *Women and Language in Literature and Society*, ed. by Sally McConnell-Ginet/Ruth Borker/Nelly Furman (New York, 1980), p. 19.
Suggested further reading on the topic of linguistic differences between men and women:
Mary Ritchie Key, "Linguistic Behavior of Male and Female," *Linguistics*, 88 (1972), 15-31.
D.G. MacKay, "Language, Thought and Social Attitudes," in: *Language: Social Psychological Perspectives*, ed. by Howard Giles/W. Peter Robinson/Philip M. Smith (New York, 1980).
Don H. Zimmermann/Candace West, "Sex Roles, Interruptions and Silences in Conversation," in: *Language and Sex: Difference and Dominance*, ed. by Barrie Thorne/Nancy Henley (Rowley, Mass.: Newbury House, 1975).

cut differentiation has evoked some criticism, too. Tannen has been reproached with side-stepping the interpretation of linguistic features, with using methods of an anthropologist rather than a linguist, basically because she relies on scenarios and anecdotes. "Tannen assumes for the most part one common culture for women, and another for men – at least in the United States. And so we are faced with essentially two sub-cultures, neither of which is differentiated internally, by reference – for example – to ethnicity or class. To what extent, we might ask, do working-class women of Asian origin from Bradford, England, for instance, occupy the same sub-culture as women from the affluent suburbs of Georgetown, USA?"[77]

In the newspaper article Adriaane Pielou sums up the main points of Tannen's book. According to Pielou men cringe especially when they are expected to talk about something personal (l. 6); they also grumble when they have been asked to do their wife a favor (l. 7); and sometimes they rage (l. 8). These verbs lack positive connotations: the body movement one associates with "to cringe" is off-putting, and "to grumble" and "to rage" show different degrees of aggressive linguistic behavior. Men, apparently, are more interested in the message than in the meta-message, which means they prefer the discussion of facts to that of feelings, and are more status-oriented (ll. 42f.). According to Tannen, they use conversations in the way of a contest to score points (l. 45), since their conception of the world is hierarchical (l. 68). So the winner is up and the loser is down, which may also read: the one who gives help (mainly the man) is up, and the one who receives help (mainly the woman) is down. This explains why men are uneasy when they have to ask for help. Moreover, men consider politeness subservient and think nothing about boasting (ll. 82f.).

According to Tannen, since women use language to create bonds between people (l. 40), they like 'we' messages; they are very much interested in the meta-message; being feeling-oriented, they discuss feelings, and they want to know every detail (l. 12). Women are used to asking for help, and attach positive connotations to it, since in their view it strengthens the bond between people (ll. 66 ff.). Women do not want to be better than others, they rather want to share a feeling of solidarity (ll. 84f.), and so they never boast (l. 86).

The meta-message is the message beyond the message. It is implicit rather than explicit; it is connotative rather than denotative. According to Tannen, another way of looking at meta-messages is to compare them to picture frames, since they frame a conversation as picture frames provide a context for the elements in the picture. "Sociologist Erving Goffman uses the term alignment to express this aspect of framing. [...] A protective gesture from a man reinforces the traditional alignment by which men protect women. But a protective gesture from a woman suggests a different scenario: one in which women protect children."[78]

Pielou quotes the following exchange between a husband and his wife as a detailed example of how the framing or alignment of the meta-message supplement the message:

message:	**meta-message:**
I'm sure we came down this street ten minutes ago. (l. 52)	I'm irritated and worry about not being in time for the party.
No, this is right. I know where I'm going. (l. 53)	Leave me alone. I'm perfectly capable of finding my way.
Should't we just stop and ask someone? (l. 54)	We'll never get there if we don't.
There's no point ... off in the wrong direction. (ll. 55 ff.)	I'm a capable person, and everybody else is stupid.
Well, even if ... we could always ask someone else. (ll. 58f.)	Why are you so afraid of asking someone. This is getting quite ridiculous.
Look, if you don't like the way I'm driving why don't you walk to ... (ll. 60f.)	Why don't you shut up and mind your own business?

From the linguistic devices used in Pilou's text it becomes quite obvious that it is a summarized interview. The author uses "says (American sociologist) Deborah Tannen" three times (ll. 2f., 15, 62), and the equivalent tense is the present. There are ellipses like "Eavesdropping [...] all in the name of research." (ll. 33 ff.), "Long-winded?" (l. 75), "For instance" (l. 94), etc., as if Pielou was still under the impression of the interview. There are also imperatives directed at the reader: Check the dialogue (l. 51), Take politeness (l. 81). All of these devices contribute to create a rather vivid, racy style.

---

[77] See *Language and Social Life*, ed. by Martin Montgomery and Helen Reid-Thomas (London: The British Council, 1994), p. 36.

[78] Deborah Tannen, *You Just Don't Understand. Men and Women in Conversation* (London: Virago, 1992), pp. 33f.

15 | David Cohen "A Gender for Change"

text type: expository text
length: 784 words
degree of difficulty: **; 34 annotations and 2 explanations
theme: male responses to recent feminist challenges
teaching points: losses and gains for men and women in their working and private lives; principles of job sharing; agenda for change

related visual material: photo of happy couple; poster "To Volvo"

for additional background material see Information Sheet: "Suggestions for the Restructuring of Work"

Background

In the discussion of the gender question a man's point of view marks the end of this anthology of texts. Are his suggestions and ideas the final stages or could they be – if not a new beginning – at least an outlook into a better future? The answer to this question is not simple and will most probably depend on the position of the addressee in the gender context. There is the homophonic aspect of the title to be considered, i.e. a gender/agenda for change (homophones = words which sound the same, but are different in spelling, meaning, and origin). An agenda is a list of the subjects to be dealt with or talked about at a meeting. What is to be on the agenda for change? Cohen's suggestions are multifold and will not only become clear from his overviews of the past and present situations, but also from his suggestions for re-structuring work (Info Sheet "Suggestions for the Restructuring of Work"). Students will and should add their ideas as to what must be on the agenda for a better future, in the sense of a better relationship between the sexes and a more just distribution of gender roles.

Cohen is an intellectual and not only conciliatory, but constructive. For his own life, he has found a *modus vivendi*, which includes his ex-wife Aileen and their two sons. "Aileen and I live in different houses now, half a mile apart. The children come to me on Sunday afternoon and stay till Tuesday morning. In order to be a practical and present father I've done what I once told myself was impossible; I've rescheduled my work. I organize things so as to have plenty of time on Monday to be back when they get in from school. Or nearly always. Ironically, it's no longer necessary. Nicholas is 16 and Reuben is 13. [...] I wish I had been around more when the children were younger but I believed, as men are conditioned to believe, that I couldn't take the risk of neglecting work. That feeling wasn't all illusion. Getting work becomes easier with time, contacts, and confidence. At 25, everyone asks you to prove that you can write an article or make a film. By the age of 35, if you are still fighting those particular battles, something has not worked out right."[79] Because of his own experiences (and mistakes) Cohen has become an ardent advocate of job sharing and the re-structuring of work (cf. Information Sheet).

Must we draw the conclusion that the gender situation is easier for intellectuals because they have more resources to draw upon, and are more conscious of their rights and possibilities? Are David Cohen and his ex-wife more privileged and therefore more willing to compromise than Mr and Mrs Jones? Or have the Cohens simply learned from the mistakes they made in the past? There are differences and exceptions in any group of society, but, as has been stated before, race and class must not be underestimated as complications of the gender issue.

Even though we have come a long way, we are nowhere close to an ideal society. Will there ever be one?

Awareness

Utopianism goes back to Thomas More and his *Utopia* (1516). It deals with the perfect society that is nowhere, but it also deals with "the ultimates of good and evil, virtue and vice".[80] In the two centuries after More, utopia functioned as a critical political and moral standard by which to judge the institutions and practices of European societies. In the 19th century, fired by the promise of the Industrial and French Revolutions, men strove to realize utopia here on earth. There were practical utopian experiments, as in Robert Owen's new New Lanark in Scotland and the Owenite New Harmony colony in Indiana. There were fictional utopias which were converted into actual utopian communities in the New World of America, itself regarded by many in a utopian light. And there were utopian social philosophies, such as those of Saint-Simon, Fourier, Comte, and Marx.[81]

When students think of a modern utopia concerning gender relationships, they might speculate about equality and shared responsibilities, just allocations in the division of labour, etc. Some students – depending on their position in the gender spectrum – might also visualise matriarchy substituting patriarchy, or a new distribution of roles, in which the social construction of gender is seen as more significant than the biologically based distinction between men and women. Whatever students come up with, they ought to be taken seriously and their ideas ought to be discussed without inhibition.

---

[79] David Cohen, *Being a Man* (London: Routledge, 1990), p. 190
[80] See introduction to the Yale edition, St. Thomas More, *Utopia*, ed. by Edward Surtz, S. J. (New Haven and London: Yale University Press, 1964), p. vii
[81] *The Fontana Dictionary of Modern Thought* (London: Fontana, 1988), pp. 888f.

The Text

The Glorious Revolution of 1688–89 was by no means a revolution in the true meaning of the word, one of the reasons being that it was bloodless. The latter is also true for the 'revolution' of 1968, despite its demos and street battles, which caused a lot of uproar, brought about some social and political changes, but none along the gender lines. It is an open secret that the heroes of the late 1960s held anything but feminist beliefs. Inspite of being confronted with a number of adversities, feminists have still managed – according to Cohen – to make the justice of their cause clear (ll. 7–11).

In their struggle feminists have faced opposition from various quarters, some more fierce than others. By and large, Cohen distinguishes among three groups of men, with reactions ranging from antagonism to understanding:

(1) insecure diehard machos (ll. 15f.), who need their macho attitudes to cover up their insecurity; to this group must be counted "large numbers of angry, sneering, or frightened men" (ll. 85f.), who object to change; Cohen claims, however, that even masculine heroes have changed their style;

(2) men who are willing to change and slowly changing; their psychological situation is determined by the experience that their masculinity is still intact, even if they look after their children or show feelings (ll. 88 ff.);

(3) trade unionists and their leaders, who, even though they belong to Britain's main left-wing organization and supposedly share some political ideals with the women's movement, feel they have too much to lose (ll. 57 ff.); they are treated with irony by the author.

From Cohen's description of the three categories of men it becomes quite evident that he is on the side of women, even though he does not see the achievements of feminists uncritically. He accepts feminism as a necessary and just social vector of force, but he criticizes that feminists have antagonized their opponents, when they could have looked for solidarity among sympathetic men (ll. 66 ff.) to help promote their cause. He voices his understanding for the reasons why women became hostile to men, even though their real enemy was patriarchy (ll. 71 ff.), but he thinks that the situation has surpassed the "battle of the sexes" (l. 80) tactics – which puts humanity into two hostile camps – and that time is ripe for something new and more conciliatory, i.e. reaching out and doing things together (ll. 91 ff.). But even though he is in favour of negotiating and re-negotiating the role distribution in individual families, e.g. who is the bread-winner, who looks after the children, etc., Cohen is completely aware of the fact that this can only be ultimately successful, if it goes beyond the limits of what individual couples can do. Political changes are necessary and that is why an official initiative is called for. Cohen's achievement is that he takes the gender issues from the well-known confines of individuality and puts them into a wider social and political context.

One of the truisms in this cluster of conflicts is, of course, that "if the oppressed are to win freedom, the oppressors must lose power" (ll. 71f.). For this reason it seems a good idea to make a list of the losses and gains of both sexes. Men have lost their superiority and their macho image. Working class men and their leaders have too much to lose anyway. On the other hand, men have emotionally gained from their contact with children and from their new courage to show feelings. Women have gained – at least partly – equal rights, equal pay, and equal opportunities, but due to their antagonistic tactics they have lost some men as allies. The conclusion that Cohen (who is presumably either a moderate left-winger or a Liberal Democrat in his political ideas) draws from all of this is that men and women should work together more and turn what they are fighting for into a common cause. We still have a long way to go, but there is also some reason for optimism.

Info Sheet 1: "Why She Became He"

Since the 80s 5,000 transsexuals have undergone sex-change operations in Britain: 75% male to female, 25% female to male. Linda became Sean six years before the publication of the following article. At 35, Sean lives as a gay man with his long-term partner James, 40. Sean works in publishing, James is a civil servant. (All names have been changed.) (Linda/Sean, *"Why She Became He"*, The Sunday Times, 23 April 1995)

The medical term for transsexuality is "gender dysphoria". For me it feels more like gender euphoria. At last there is a feeling of being completely at home with the way I look and who I am. Becoming a man was the most positive step ever taken in my life.

From the age of about five, I felt uncomfortable as a girl. All the things that boys did somehow felt so natural. I loved football, war films and space exploration. I found myself looking at men on television or in the street and feeling a strong identification with their masculinity. Wearing girls' clothes made me feel extremely self-conscious, and I still remember throwing the only doll I was ever given out of the window. Instead I would spend hours playing with Dinky cars and plastic soldiers. Although I was a very pretty little girl, I saw myself as a little boy. Even then, part of me knew that I would never grow up to be a woman.

By the time I reached my teens, I was the tallest girl in the school. Nobody ever picked on me, because one word was enough to shut them up. There was a feeling of being different from the crowd, but I enjoyed that. Going off to university gave me a golden opportunity to begin expressing the androgynous side of my personality. The 1970s was a time when students could experiment with gender and fashion as much as they liked and nobody even blinked. I started dressing as a man in clothes modelled on The Beatles and all my friends thought I was the epitome of style. [...]

The decision to change sex is not one you take lightly. It took me until the age of 29. For a while I was happy with what appeared to be the best of both worlds, but there was a horror of growing older being neither one thing nor another. I wanted to become a real man with a deep voice and flat chest. [After the operations] it was becoming increasingly important to make everything official – to change from a female to a male name by deed poll and to have my new name on my passport, cheque books, credit cards and all my personal papers. The only document a transsexual cannot legally change is his or her birth certificate. [...]

By far the most difficult aspect of changing sex was adjusting to the altered social expectations and perceptions now that I was a man. You suddenly realise that you are not supposed to sit tight if somebody needs a hand moving heavy furniture. Even in the days of post-feminism, men are still expected to be far more assertive and pushy than women. Pouring out your innermost feelings to other men is simply not on. There is a certain male banter that you hear in pubs and offices, and I had to quickly pick up the art of making idle chatter about sport and cars. Other men began relating to me in a way that made me realise I had finally become one of the "blokes".[82]

---

[82] An interesting novel dealing with the topic of transsexuality is Rose Tremain, *Sacred Country* (London: Hodder & Stoughton, 1993).

Info Sheet 2: "What Little Girls Are Really Made of ..."

... sugar and spite and plenty of fight. In her article "What Little Girls Are Really Made of" (The Observer, 4 February 1996) *Katharine Whitehorn ponders on the reasons why women are getting so aggressive and violent.*

My mother brought me up to believe that no women were as foul as some men; a useful working guideline for life. There is now a growing worry, though, that women are doing their best to catch up. Studies from the University of Michigan suggest that role models such as *Thelma and Louise, Charlie's Angels, Wonder Woman* and other rough stuff are making girls grow up as aggressive as men. And late-night TV shows in which beefcake males cavort for the delectation of hordes of screaming females assume that they are also supposed to be as crude about sex as the most dickheaded stud. Is this, as some are claiming, feminism carried to its ultimate and disgusting conclusion, or is something else at work here?

Women seem more aggressive than they used to be, certainly: their crime rate is rising faster than men's. Elizabeth Hurley was mugged by a group of girls; and a programme on girl gangs in Manchester had one of the Fallow Field Ladies cheerfully remarking: 'It's just something to do – once you do it the first time it's easy.' They described bashing up a woman for her money: 'Everyone was, like, enjoying doing it.' They seem to do it for the same reasons boys do – for excitement, for the feeling of belonging in a group, for money and to avoid being a victim, too. In a tough situation, women will behave violently: at the turn of the century in Glasgow the saying was: 'Come doon the close, there's a couple of ladies fighting like tigers' – with razors it would have been then.

If girls are bolder, cruder, more sexually upfront and violent with it, it is normal to blame TV and film. No doubt males and females both are desensitised to violence by watching the endless stream of fights and shoot-outs on TV. But rather than behaviour being changed by the mere fact of seeing girls with guns, it's more likely that TV picks up on what it thinks is s trend. [...]

I have no wish, believe me, to be reassuring. I can't buy the idea that we have always been as violent as we are now, that we are simply more aware of it these days. Doctors and teachers didn't get knocked about by their patients and pupils and pupils' families; time was, shops didn't have to be boarded up near football matches; guns and drugs simply weren't around. There are all sorts of 'causes of crime' – boredom, unemployment, poverty but most of all having no sense of identity or purpose elsewhere – and that affects girls too. No doubt women broke out less when they were more tightly programmed into a given slot in society, protected and suppressed; now that they're not particularly protected, they aren't prepared to be suppressed either.

But if there is more uncivilised behaviour among girls, I'm convinced that it's not just because we have stopped confining them to womanly roles. It is because we have lost confidence in the whole idea of civilising anybody. We don't think we should be forcing our young into any particular mould. [...]

It used to be assumed that women would be the civilising influence – a noble thought. But a woman can't do it on her own, without a family network, without some sort of sanctions, without a strong and involved father. A father, to give a son an idea of how man should behave, doubtless; but also to admire and appreciate a daughter, if only as a counterweight to the views of the boyfriend and other girls. How is it, by the way, that when the shortcomings of the young Windsors are discussed, the role of the Queen as mother is endlessly chewed over, but no one ever seems to mention Prince Philip? Well, at least the younger royals don't mug women in the street.

Perhaps the real reason we are all so horrified at the idea of girls behaving badly is not that we are more scared of being mugged by them than by their brothers; it is that society has always counted on women to tame the brothers, and now they're not doing it. Tough. But reposing morality in women only was probably always a mistake; they too, after all, are members of the human race.[87]

---

[87] A number of organisations have been established in Britain which help the families of adolescent bullies and their victims, e.g. The Anti-Bullying Campaign, Kidscape, Parents Against Bullying or Education Otherwise.

Info Sheet 3: Role cards for role play on "Do we need girls' schools?"

Role card A
You are to be the new headmistress of a school in an area where parents are cooperative and interested in the academic opportunities of their children. You have got progressive pedagogic ideas. You believe in co-education, but you also want to give girls a better chance in the natural sciences. You are in favor of single-sex classes in those subjects and voice your opinion very decidedly.

Role card B
You are a male school governor. You are fairly conservative. You think that a mixture of co-educational and single-sex classes is an unworkable idea, which will only cause administrative problems. You voice your opinion in favor of co-education and try to win the others over to your side by stressing its psychological advantages. You claim that single-sex classes are a step back in school administration.

Role card C
You are a female parent. You have got a 15-year-old daughter who you want to attend this new school in your area. You want to give your child the best education within your financial means. Your child is good at languages, and interested in natural sciences, but you fear she will be overwhelmed by male competition in her class. So you strongly support the headmistress's pedagogic approach.

Role card D
You are a male school governor. You are broad-minded and progressive. You know the latest trends in education and you think that good opportunities in education can only be provided at single-sex schools. In addition to that you see the same administrative problems as your colleague if single-sex and co-educational classes are established. So you plead in favor of a single-sex school, because you believe that the idea of co-education is uneconomical.

Role card E
You are a devoted language teacher. Your subject is German. You cannot understand why foreign languages do not play a more important role in the curriculum. That is why you raise the question why everybody is so worried about the fact that girls are not successful enough at mathematics, and nobody worries about the fact that boys are not successful enough at foreign languages. You are in favour of co-education, but you want more male participants in your German classes.

Info Sheet 4: The Distillers, "Seneca Falls"

Oh its set in 1848 in the crush of New York state
and the thing about destiny is it never ever makes mistakes

Susan B. Anthony
Forever haunting me
Owned raped sold thrown
A woman was never her own

They cried freedom rise up for me

I want i want i want freedom

Oh its set in 1848 in the crush of New York state
and the thing about destiny is it never ever sets you free

Elizabeth Cady
Forever reminding me
I dont steal the air i breathe

Freedom rise up for me

www.plyrics.com

Special thanks to Birthe Dobertin and Ann-Kristin Lange for their suggestion of the above song.

Info Sheet 5: Historical Development of the Women's Rights Movements in the U.S. and Britain

History provides many individual examples of women with power, courage and talent, such as aristocratic ladies, saints, scientists, writers and artists. But they stand out as exceptions who did not improve the status of ordinary women. It took a very long time before feminism started, and women began to organize themselves.

U.S.

First wave:

- mid 19th cent.: the abolitionist struggle (e.g. in the Anti-Slavery Society, founded on 4 December, 1833 in Philadelphia; it influences white female campaigners immensely, since in their fight for the abolition of slavery they realize that they are denied equal rights, too) and the women's rights movement lead to the Seneca Falls Convention (1848) [= era of feminist pioneers];
- September 1868: Working Woman's Association is founded to stress the importance of organizing female workers in the otherwise male chauvinist labor movement;
- 1869: American Woman Suffrage Association (AWSA) [conservatives] and National Woman's Suffrage Association (NWSA) [radical feminists] are founded; both associations agree on the desirability of the vote, but not on the reasons why it is desirable; the conservatives are content to work within the male power structure; the radicals see the vote as a symbol of the political power they want to achieve in the long run;
- 1890: merger of the two into the National American Woman Suffrage Association (NAWSA); it entails a strengthening of the conservative forces;
- the 1870s and 80s: are characterized by 'social purity' feminism, based on Evangelical principles (alcohol, violence, and sexual excess are seen as masculine evils; women are considered to be morally superior, purer, and not ruled by animal passions);
- 1920: Amendment XIX is passed; it grants suffrage to women.

Second wave:

- 1964: The Civil Rights Act forbids discrimination. The Equal Employment Opportunities Act leads to affirmative action [employment of minority groups];
- 1965: National Organization of Women (NOW) is founded by Betty Friedan [stress is on equality with men, esp. in legal and employment contexts];
- 1970: Equal Pay Act;
- 1972: Equal Rights Amendment Bill outlaws sex discrimination;
- 1973: the Roe v. Wade Supreme Court decision gives women the right to choose an abortion.

Britain

First wave:

- mid 19th cent.: the Industrial Revolution and the wealth of the British Empire has created an army of working women (mill-girls, domestic servants, farm labourers, milliners, seamstresses, governesses);
- 1840: International Anti-Slavery Convention; it is a major issue, whether female delegates from the U.S. should be allowed to take part;
- 1856: petitions are collected for a Married Woman's Property Bill (a wife's right to keep her own property and income);

- 1870: there is a Parliamentary majority for a women's enfranchisement Bill, which would have become law but for the opposition of the Liberal leader W.E. Gladstone;
- 1901: the cotton workers' petition is taken to Westminster; the campaign is organized by female cotton workers, who exclusively work through labour and industrial organizations; they are peaceful, non-militant, but radical (stronghold Lancashire);
- 1903: Women's Social and Political Union (WSPU) is founded by Emmeline Pankhurst (1858–1928); its members organize a militant, sometimes even violent suffrage campaign, culminating in arrests, hunger strikes and force-feeding;
- 1918: Representation of the People Act extends franchise to women over 30, who are householders;
- 1928: Representation of the People Act realizes democratic universal suffrage.

Second wave:

The women's civil rights movement in the U.S. influences the dicussion in Britain:
- 1970: Equal Pay Act (effective in 1975); necessitates equal pay for equal work;
- 1975: Sex Discrimination Act (makes discrimination on the basis of sex unlawful in employment, education, provision of housing, goods, facilities and services, and advertising);
- 1978: Finance Act (women who pay taxes on a pay as you earn basis are entitled to their own tax rebates).

Info Sheet 6: Main Tendencies in the Women's Movement

1. Developments 1970–79

Radical feminists:
They see patriarchy as the main problem, i.e. a whole system of male power over women (male rulers, male military, industrial, political, and religious establishments, male trade unions, and the male-dominated left) reinforcing and being reinforced by the power of individual men over women and children in their families.

They stress women only campaigns and demonstrations, building a woman's space and a woman's culture.

Socialist feminists:
They see a combination of male domination **and** class exploitation as the main problem, and fight against both. They feel that real liberation is impossible as long as power and wealth in the world is monopolized by a tiny minority.

They emphasize alliances with other oppressed groups and classes, e.g. anti-imperialist movements, workers' organizations, the political parties of the left. They are engaged in permanent dialogue with progressive men in these organizations.

Liberal feminists:
They see the problem simply as one of prejudice. They claim that the system needs to be corrected, not overturned. So they think that more equal-rights legislation and more positive role models for girls are needed.

They concentrate on lobbying governments for pro-women reforms and trying to influence the decision makers.

In the very beginning, the socialist feminists predominated, since their group emerged out of the social protests and anti-Vietnam war movement of the late 1960s. By the end of the 1970s, the radical feminists had grown more influential.[83]

2. Developments in the 1990s

In the 1990s there has been a growing together of different positions into a synthesis that recognizes some of the strengths and weaknesses in all three tendencies. In addition to that, there have been new developments: second-wave feminists were always interested in the relationship between biological sex and social conditioning. Some feminists tended to favour explanations of the social significance of the biological differences between men and women by referring to biological determinism, which claimed that male-female differences were innate. Others argued that gender was socially constructed. Within a short period of time, most feminists began to write and speak about gender rather than about sex, a focus of attention that looked to femininity and masculinity rather than to maleness and femaleness for explanations of gender relations. The project was to understand femininity, but it soon became apparent that this would be impossible without also considering masculinity. The focus changed from 'the woman question', which saw men as the norm and women as the 'other', to questioning why men were regarded as the norm.

A central concern is with gender acquisition. This is very much work in progress, but the most convincing explorations stress that the acquisition of gender identity is a precarious never-finished process. The insight that the acquisition of masculinity and femininity represents socially conditioned processes of developing an identity probably raises more questions about power in gender relations than it answers.[84]

---

[83] See Susan Alice Watkins, Marisa Rueda, Marta Rodriguez, *Feminism for Beginners* (Cambridge: Icon Books, 1992), pp. 120f.
[84] See Joni Lovenduski, Vicky Randall, *Contemporary Feminist Politics. Women and Power in Britain* (Oxford: Oxford University Press, 1993), pp. 84 ff.

Info Sheet 7: Suffragettes on Hunger Strike in Holloway

Sylvia is the daughter of Emmeline Pankhurst and sister to Christabel. Starting off as fundamental advocates of women's suffrage they became increasingly polarized into two mutually antagonistic factions: the Women's Social and Political Union led by Sylvia's mother Emmeline and by her sister Christabel (which was essentially conservative) and Sylvia's East London Federation of the Suffragettes (which stood on the far left of the political spectrum). For further information see: Sylvia Pankhurst, *The Suffragette Movement* (London: Virago, 1977), pp. 442f.

Rule 243A being in force, we were exempt from the search and permitted to wear our own clothes. Writing materials were not allowed, but I was well supplied with paper and pencils; I wore a bag of them round my waist, under my skirt, and had an additional thick wad of paper as a lining to my brush-and-comb tidy. As it was known that we should hunger strike, we were at once placed in hospital cells, which differed from the ordinary cells in having an ordinary bed with a spring mattress instead of the plank. In spite of the hunger and thirst strike I was able to write fairly steadily, for the greater part of most days, until near the end of my imprisonment, lying on the bed in such a position that what I was doing could not be observed through the spy hole, and always on the qui vive to conceal my work between the sheets. I kept a calendar scratched with a hairpin on the white-washed walls of my cell, and printed favourite verses there to keep myself occupied during the periods when my secret writing was likely to be interrupted. For this the governor, a tall, sandy-haired man with a long red face, several times sentenced me to various terms of 'close solitary confinement,' but as exercise and books from the library had already been withdrawn as a punishment for the hunger strike, the additional punishments were only a matter of form.[85] I permitted myself the great luxury, for such it became, of rinsing out my mouth only once a day, lest the tongue should absorb moisture. I was careful never to swallow a single drop. I was always cold, but I felt only a trace of hunger, and less as the days passed. Thirst strikers crave only for water. Food such as I had never before seen in Holloway[86] was daily placed in my cell: chicken, Brand's essence, fruit. The varied colours diverted my eyes in the drabness of the cell, but I had no more inclination to eat the still life groups on my table than if they had been a painting or a vase of flowers. Nevertheless the first night I took the precaution of putting the eatables on the floor under the table, with a stool in front, in case I should go to them in my sleep; then realized the absurdity of such measures, for I could not sleep.

On the third day the two doctors sounded my heart and felt my pulse. The senior told me he had no alternative but to feed me by force.

---

[85] Soon afterwards the Liberal government introduced the "Cat and Mouse Act" (official term: The Prisoners' Temporary Discharge for Ill Heath Bill), which enabled the authorities to release women on hunger strike when their health deteriorated only to re-arrest them when they had recovered sufficiently.

[86] Holloway was and still is a prison for women in London.

Gender Roles – Resource Book

Info Sheet 8: The Diary of Samuel Pepys

Biographical information:
Samuel Pepys was born in London on 23 February 1633. His father was a needy tailor, living off Fleet Street; his mother had been a domestic servant. Pepys became a scholar at Magdalene College, Cambridge in 1650, and took his degree in 1653. In 1655 he married a girl of fifteen, Elizabeth, who was as poor as Pepys himself. Pepys's connection with Lord Montagu secured him his entry into the Navy Office, which resulted in his keeping his famous diary. He would frequently keep late hours at the Navy Office and write the day's doings in his journal by candlelight. He voiced complaints of eye trouble, owing to which he had to abandon his diary on 31 May 1669. The diary, which was not deciphered till 1825, was written in shorthand, with neat and small signs in the early volumes, but the quality of his script decreasing in the later volumes. Pepys died in 1703. The following are exerpts from *The Diary of Samuel Pepys*. 1660–1669, ed. by O.F. Morshead (London: G.Bell and Sons, 1927), pp. 137f., 204f., 238.

31 Dec. 1662
At noon took my wife to Mrs Pierce's by invitacion [sic] to dinner, where there came Dr Clerke and his wife and sister and Mr Knight, chief chyrurgeon to the King and his wife. We were pretty merry, the two men being excellent company, but I confess I am wedded from the opinion either of Mrs Pierce's beauty upon discovery of her naked neck to-day, being undrest when we came in, or of Mrs Clerke's genius, which I so much admired, I finding her to be so conceited and fantastique in her dress this day and carriage, though the truth is, witty enough. After dinner with much ado the doctor and I got away to follow our business for a while, he to his patients and I to the Tangier Committee, where the Duke of York was. Thence Mr Povy (Treasurer of the Duke of York), in his coach carried Mr Gauden and I into London to Mr Bland's, the merchant, where we staid discoursing. Then to eat a dish of anchovies and drink wine and syder, and very merry, but above all things pleased to hear Mrs Bland talk like a merchant in her husband's business very well, and it seems she do understand it and perform a great deal. [...]

Thus ends this year with great mirth to me and my wife. [...] Our home at the Navy-office, which is and has a pretty while been in good condition, finished and made very convenient. My purse is worth £ 650, besides my goods of all sorts, which yet might have been more but for my late layings out upon my house and public assessment, and yet would not have been so much if I had not lived a very orderly life all this year by virtue of the oaths that God put into my heart to take against wine, plays, and other expenses, and to observe for these last twelve months, and which I am now going to renew, I under God owing my present content thereunto. My family is myself and wife, William, my clerk; Jane, my wife's upper mayde, but, I think, growing proud and negligent upon it: we must part, which troubles me; Susan, our cook-mayde, a pretty willing wench, but no good cook; and Wayneman, my boy, who I am now turning away for his naughty tricks. [...]

8 Mar. 1664
Up with some little discontent with my wife upon her saying that she had got and used some puppy-dog water, being put upon it by a desire of my aunt Wight to get some for her, who hath a mind, unknown to her husband, to get some for her ugly face. [...]

31 Dec. 1664
So ends the old yeare, I bless God, with great joy to me. I bless God I never have been in so good plight as to my health in so very cold weather as this is, nor indeed in any hot weather, these ten years as I am at this day and have been this four or five months. But I am at a great losse to know whether it be my hare's foote (a charm against the colic), or taking every morning of a pill of turpentine, or my having left off the wearing of a gowne. [...]

Some of these superstitious medical and/or cosmetic ideas are parallelled in text 4 of the *Students' Book*.

Info Sheet 9: Role Cards

One of the following sets of role cards may be used for Project 12, text 8:

Role card A
You are a social worker responsible for the inmates of a prison. The son is kept there on detention. In your conversations with the son you have found out that he is emotionally disturbed. You want to find out his family background. So you go and visit the mother.

Role card B
You are the mother whose son is detained for having killed three men. The social worker who is in contact with your son visits you and asks you a lot of questions about your past and your relationship with your son.

Role card A1
You are a renowned court psychiatrist who has been heard in number of difficult legal cases.
You have been asked to give your assessment of the mental state of the son. So you visit him in prison in order to find out about his background and his present state of mind. You also want to find out about his relationship to his mother.

Role card B1
You are the son. You are detained because you have been accused of triple murder.
The court psychiatrist who has been asked to write a medical certificate about you, visits you. He/She asks a lot of questions about the deed and also about yourself. You can either be co-operative or withdrawn.

Info Sheet 10: Suggestions for the Restructuring of Work

The following ideas have been put forth by David Cohen, *Being a Man* (London: Routledge, 1990), p. 194.

The social psychologist Marie Jahoda (1981) has shown that, in our organization of society at least, going to work provides structure and a way of passing time. The unemployed suffer. But there is a big difference between organizing your life around work (which is what we do now [...]) and fitting necessary work into the rest of your life which has at least equal importance. [...] Taking leisure seriously for men, means being less involved and less invested in work. It means taking less competitive pleasure out of it. It means examining and seeing what they stand to gain out of following issues:

1. Equal training for women.
2. Equal pay so that it will be economically easier for women to spend time working.
3. More flexible career structures so that you don't get stuck or bypassed for promotion if you take time off to look after children and/or house.
4. Proper funding for proper child-minding arrangements. The continued failure of governments of all complexions to provide adequate facilities is scandalous.
5. Some analysis of the age structure by which we organize work. At present, the time when men are supposed to concentrate most on their careers – from the age of 25 to 45, say – is the period when family stresses are likely to be highest. What kind of jobs might give more opportunity from 40 onwards? Industrial psychologists argue that we waste executives after 40 and deny them all kind of chances. It is worth considering what happened if men and women had a chance to share jobs or do part time jobs while their children were small knowing that, after 40, they had good job opportunities. More employment prospects for the over forties might make sharing child care easier.

There is a need of serious discussion and initiatives on job-sharing. This often appeared a radical fancy, but men do stand to gain much by way of the quality of their life especially through having more time for themselves.

Info Sheet 11: Glossary

The following glossary can be used for fast reference, but also for linguistic work, e.g. the rewriting of texts or a consideration of what equivalents exist for the English expressions in your own language.

affirmative action
The term describes government policies which give preferential treatment to particular social groups – for instance, to gain access to education and employment – on the grounds that the accumulated consequences of past discrimination or disadvantage require and justify such a remedy. The idea was developed in the U.S. in the 1970s, and is a continuing source of political conflict. Opponents of affirmative action policies, which they prefer to call "reverse discrimination" in order to replace the positive connotations of the original phrase, regard them as unjust in that they allegedly discriminate against individuals outside the preferred group, who are themselves not personally responsible for the group's disadvantages. In practice, the conflict is on racial lines, although some conflict also turns on affirmative action for women.

feminine
The term refers to the qualities generally considered to be womanly, e.g. gentleness and prettiness.

gender
It is incorrect and misleading to use the terms of 'sex' and 'gender' interchangeably. 'Sex' describes biological functions – such as producing eggs or sperm – while 'gender' should be seen as a purely cultural phenomenon, such as the accumulation of information and behaviour patterns that are passed on from generation to generation.

gender dysphoria
It is a term for the unhappiness or discomfort experienced by one whose sexual organs do not match one's gender identity.

gender identity
The term denotes one's psychological gender role: masculine or feminine.

gender role
It is a set of rules that define what clothing, forms of behaviour, thoughts, feelings, relationships, etc., are considered appropriate or inappropriate for members of each sex.

masculine
The term refers to the qualities that are generally considered to be typical of or suitable for men, such as strength, authority and a deep voice.

matriarchy
The term means authority exercised by women over men. It is often used more loosely to refer to female autonomy, mother-right, recognition of female principle, worship of goddess, matrilineage, women-centred social organization, etc.

patriarchy
The term describes authority and control exercised by men over women. The concept is used by feminists to refer to what is perceived to be a fundamental and universal state of male dominance.

role behaviour
The term refers to the ways of acting which are expected of a person playing a particular social role.

role expectations
Most social interactions involve dealing with other people in a particular way, because the relationship is one which is recognised by society, and for which there are established norms of behaviour. Each social situation that we are in carries its own particular set of expectations about the "proper" way to behave. Social norms set the kind of behaviour that is acceptable.

role groupings

Roles are an important way in which society organises itself. Generally speaking, five different sorts of role groupings, which all have their appropriate roles and role behaviour, have been identified. The five groupings are:
- age and sex groupings, such as infant, old man, boy, woman;
- family groupings, such as father, aunt, grandmother;
- status groupings, such as chairperson, supervisor, manager, shop steward;
- occupational groupings, such as teacher, lawyer, car worker, secretary;
- common interest groupings, such as sports club member, pub local, video-game enthusiast.

sexual discrimination

The term refers to the unfair treatment of people because of their sex, usually the unfair treatment of women. Sexual discrimination is illegal in Britain and the U.S., and people and companies can be taken to court if it is thought that they are guilty of it.

sexual harassment

Lists of specific offences vary greatly. A general definition describes it as unwanted sexual attention that makes a person feel uncomfortable or causes problems in school or at work, or in social settings.

wedding

Of course, there are different, even contradictory attitudes to it. The Politically Correct Guide to Sex and Dating advises: Women, if you feel you must get married, you owe it to society – if not to yourself – to avoid a standard ceremony. This advice is offered by feminist scholars, who note that it is important, "not to perpetuate the public symbolic meaning of heterosexism and women being the legal possession of men." "Private ceremonies of commitment" or legal contracts are permissible, since they do not carry the same patriarchal and heterosexual interpretation.

A wedding is a marriage ceremony, traditionally with a party or meal following it, in Britain people tend to have a **wedding breakfast** for the family and friends. Although it is called a breakfast, the meal is a lunch or dinner. The **wedding reception** is a party held after the ceremony, usually by the married couple or the bride's parents.

In Britain people get married either in church or in a registry office. In the U.S. people get married in a hotel, the office of the justice of the peace or a wedding chapel, which is purpose-built for wedding ceremonies.

Important people at the wedding are the **bride and bridegroom** or groom. The bridegroom is not supposed to see the bride on the day of the wedding until they meet in church as this is considered to be bad luck. The man has a male friend with him, called the **best man**, and the bride has got some female friends called **bridesmaids**. The bridegroom arrives at the church first and waits inside near the altar with the best man. Just before the wedding ceremony begins, the bride arrives in a car with her father. It is the custom for the bride's father to **'give her away'** (= officially to 'give' her to the bridegroom). The bride and her father walk slowly up the aisle of the church, with the bridesmaids. People sometimes talk about **'walking up the aisle'** when they mean 'getting married'.

During the service the bridegroom gives the bride a wedding ring and says, "With this ring I thee wed". The priest or minister asks the bride and the bridegroom in turn, "Will you have this man/woman to be your wedded husband/wife – for better or for worse?" The bride and bridegroom each say "I will". At the end of the ceremony the priest or minister says, "I pronounce you man and wife", which means that they are officially married. The bride and bridegroom then sign the register (= a special book which is the official record of their marriage).

After the reception the married couple begin their **honeymoon**.

Info Sheet 12: Nursery Rhymes

Nursery rhymes offer a wide field of differences concerning the role expectations of girls and boys, even though one frequently has to read between the lines. Compare the following:

Mädchen, die pfeifen, und Hähnen, die krähen, soll man beizeiten den Hals umdrehen.

Georgie Porgie, pudding and pie, kissed all the girls and made them cry.

Mary, Mary, quite contrary, how does your garden grow? With silver bells and cockle shells, and pretty maids in a row.

Little Polly Flinders sat among the cinders, warming her pretty little toes, her mother came and caught her, and whipped her little daughter, for spoiling her nice new clothes.

Little Jack Horner, sat in the corner, eating a Christmas pie; he put in his thumb and pulled out a plum, and said "What a good boy am I"!

The Queen of Hearts she made some tarts, all on a summer's day; the Knave of Hearts he stole the tarts, and took them clean away.